HOMAGE TO PAUL CELAN

edited by G.C. Waldrep
and Ilya Kaminsky

HOMAGE TO
PAUL CELAN

edited by G.C. Waldrep
and Ilya Kaminsky

MARICK PRESS

Library of Congress Cataloguing in Publication Data

Ilya Kaminsky and G.C Waldrep
Homage to Paul Celan
Essays. Non-Fiction. 1ˢᵗ Paperback Edition, 2011

ISBN 10: 1-934851-35-3
ISBN 13: 978-1-934851-35-7
Copyright © by Ilya Kaminsky, 2011
Copyright © by G.C. Waldrep, 2011
Copyright © by Marick Press, 2011
Design and typesetting by Really Big Robot
Cover design by Really Big Robot
Printed and bound in the United States

Marick Press
P.O. Box 36253, Grosse Pointe Farms, Michigan 48236
www.marickpress.com
Mariela Griffor, Publisher
Distributed by spdbooks.org, and Ingram

Marick Press is an independent literary press that publishes fine literature.
Marick Press is a registered 501 (c) 3 non-profit organization and we rely on
public and private funding to carry out the mission of publishing annually 6-
8 titles in both hardcover and paperback covering a broad spectrum of topic
that range from literary non-fiction, creative non-fiction, poetry, fiction and
reprint of previously published titles.

Marick Press is not-for-profit literary publisher, founded to preserve the best
work by poets around the world, including many under published women
poets.

Marick Press seeks out and publishes the best new work from an eclectic
range of aesthetics —work that is technically accomplished, distinctive in
style, and thematically fresh.

CONTENTS

GOD OF ROOMS

Jean Valentine

god of rooms, of this room made of taken away
papers and books, of removal, this single
room made of taken-away
empty now, god of empty rooms, god of
one unable to speak, god of turned-over boats
in the wind (god of boat and mouth and ear)
listen to someone, be of-you
needful to someone

INTRODUCTION

OF STRANGENESS THAT WAKES US
Ilya Kaminsky

If there is a country named Celania—as Julia Kristeva
once proposed—its holy texts are filled with doubt, and they
overcome this doubt almost successfully, with words of wrenching,
uncompromised beauty.

If there is such a country, Celania's traditions aren't much
different from the notion proposed by Islam: the first word that was
revealed to the prophet was *Igra* (Read!). Perhaps in Celania, as
in the Ottoman Empire, the calligraphers delight in creating mazes
of embellishment in which the text is secreted like a treasure. The
deciphering of the text proves the worthiness of the reader.

Perhaps Celania's inhabitants know, better than inhabitants
of our world do, that we all continue to live in Biblical times. They
would also know that if one is to write poems, they might as well be
modern psalms—psalms for our very own moment in time, modern
psalms. Here is one such example:

Zurich, the Stork Inn
—*for Nelly Sachs*

Of too much was our talk, of
too little. Of the You
and You-Again, of
how clarity troubles, of
Jewishness, of
your God.

Of
that.
On the day of an ascension, the

Minister stood over there, it sent
some gold across the water.

Of your God was our talk, I spoke
against him, I
let the heart that I had
hope:
for
his highest, death-rattled, his
quarrelling word –

Your eye looked on, looked away,
your mouth
spoke its way to the eye, and I heard:

We
don't know, you know,
we don't know, do we?
what counts.

translated from the German by Michael Hamburger

As is well known, this poem describes the meeting of Celan and
Sachs, another important poet of the post-war German language.
The subject of conversation is God, and Sachs, presumably, speaks
for him; Celan speaks *against*; if one is about to speak about one's
relationship with the divine in us, one is always troubled ("of your

God was our talk, I spoke / against him, I / let the heart that I had / hope"). Clarity troubles.

"Extreme clarity is a mystery," maintains Mahmoud Darwish. Celan, often considered a difficult poet, is in this poem at his most clear. The syntax here follows the way a mind moves ("we / don't know, you know, / we don't know, do we?, / what counts"), and the mind argues with itself, in front of its God, and with its God. And finds hope, even in this "death-rattled" world.

This quarrel of intense lyricism is not something we haven't heard before. We have heard Yeats famously saying that argument with another is rhetoric while argument with oneself is poetry. We know that in *Hamlet* the Prince often addresses others in prose, but himself in verse. When in another poem Celan searches for *O One, O none, O no one, O you,* we might recall Lear's *never, never, never, never, never.*[1]

Perhaps we have lived in Celania all along. Perhaps Paul Celan's poems are psalms for our moment in time—prayers that question God even as they reach for God.

*

The orchestration and wreckage of syntax in original German imposes itself on a receiving language (here, English), and the reader of Celan in translation (however distant it may be from the original) finds something fresh in this dismantling of the lyric in English.

Why does the language appear so fresh when it is wrecked so? The best answer to this question was offered in an interview with another Eastern European poet, Zbigniew Herbert. Interviewer: "What is the purpose of poetry?" Herbert's response: "To wake up!"

---

1   "Never..." is perhaps Shakespeare's single most Celan-like line; it is the single line around which all of Lear revolves.

4

We are asleep in the language until language does not wake us with its strangeness.

How does the wreckage of language wake us? Here is an outside example, a word-by-word translation from another famous text. The language is Hebrew, and it requires us to read the passage from right to left.

בְּרֵאשִׁית, בָּרָא אֱלֹהִים, אֵת הַשָּׁמַיִם, וְאֵת הָאָרֶץ.
[and the earth] [the earth] [and] [the heavens] [God]
[created] [in the beginning]

וְהָאָרֶץ, הָיְתָה תֹהוּ וָבֹהוּ, וְחֹשֶׁךְ, עַל-פְּנֵי תְהוֹם; וְרוּחַ
[God] [and the spirit of] [deep] [upon the face of] [and
darkness] [and void] [waste] [was]

מְרַחֶפֶת, עַל-פְּנֵי הַמָּיִם.
[and there was] [light] [let there be] [God] [and said] [the
waters] [upon the face of] [moved]

וַיַּרְא אֱלֹהִים אֶת-הָאוֹר, כִּי-טוֹב;
[between] [God] [and divided] [that good] [the light] [God]
   [and saw light]

These opening verses of Genesis are well known, expected even. I suggest we read it backwards:

"And the earth, the earth and the heavens God created in the beginning
God and the spirit of deep upon the face of and darkness and void
waste was

5

And there was light let there be God and said waters…"

As we look at the wreckage of this familiar text realize, once again:
we are asleep in the language—until language wakes us with its
strangeness.

What does this have to do with Celan? How does strangeness
lead to a truth that pierces us? Nabokov argued that all great
literature follows the pattern *magic, lesson*—the author seduces us
with a strange music, then teaches us a lesson. This is exactly how
the evocative, strange imagery moves towards a powerful statement
in another Celan poem:

> I hear that the bread which looks at him
> heals the hanged man,
> the bread baked for him by his wife,
>
> I hear that they call life
> our only refuge.

With Celan, the strangeness goes further, rooted in the poet's inward,
almost cryptogrammatical relationship with German, a language
whose silences are "cooked in charred hands." This wreckage, too,
is translation. As Anne Carson notes, Celan "is a poet who uses
language *as if he were always translating.*" Writing to his wife from
Germany the poet himself said, "I am not sure the German I write
in is spoken here, or anywhere." Celan's is the lyricism of privacy
(prayer is private, no matter with how many fellow congregants
it is uttered or in how many prayer books it appears)—not of
hermeticism, or of difficulty. A prayer is a private correspondence,

not a commandment.[2]

A great poet is not someone who speaks in stadiums to a thousand listeners. A great poet is a very private person. In his privacy this poet creates a language in which he is able to speak, privately, to many people at the same time.

*

There is no need to make a cult of personality out of the life or death of the poet Paul Celan.

What we want is to observe his process, to braid a "breath-rope." We want to see how his belief that "attentiveness is the natural prayer of the human soul" applies to his handling of words "as if they had the density of objects"[3]—to his syntax, line-breaks, images. If the original Greek meaning of the word *Eros* is to stand outside one's self, then what do we make of this voice that stands outside of the language in which it psalms? "Celan's language," Pierre Joris writes,

> though German on the surface, is a foreign language, even
> for native speakers. The Celanian dynamic...involves a
> complex double movement...of love for his mother tongue
> and of...strife against her murderers who are the originators
> and carriers of that same tongue.

But how to translate one man's "solitary conversation with a German dictionary" into English? What translates *estrangement*? Can a translator teach his "hands to sleep" in another tongue? Here is John

---

2   Or, to quote Jabès: "The word of God is not commandment but correspondence."

3   This is Paul Auster's phrase, echoing George Steiner.

7

Felstiner's attempt:

Deathfugue

Black milk of daybreak we drink it at evening
we drink it at midday and morning we drink it at night
we drink and we drink
we shovel a grave in the air there you won't lie too cramped
A man lives in the house he plays with his vipers he writes
he writes when it grows dark to Deutschland your golden
   hair Margareta
he writes it and steps out of doors and the stars are all
   sparkling, he
whistles his hounds to come close
he whistles his Jews into rows has them shovel a grave in the
   ground
he commands us to play up for the dance.
Black milk of daybreak we drink you at night
we drink you at morning and midday we drink you at
   evening
we drink and we drink
A man lives in the house he plays with his vipers he writes
he writes when it grows dark to Deutschland your golden
   hair Margareta
Your ashen hair Shulamith we shovel a grave in the air there
   you won't lie too cramped

He shouts jab the earth deeper you lot there you others sing
   up and play
he grabs for the rod in his belt he swings it his eyes are so
   blue

jab your spades deeper you lot there you others play on for
   the dancing

Black milk of daybreak we drink you at night
we drink you at midday and morning we drink you at
   evening
we drink and we drink
a man lives in the house your goldenes Haar Margareta
your aschenes Haar Shulamith he plays his vipers
He shouts play death more sweetly this Death is a master
   from Deutschland
he shouts scrape your strings darker you'll rise then as
   smoke to the sky
you'll have a grave then in the clouds there you won't lie too
   cramped

Black milk of daybreak we drink you at night
we drink you at midday Death is a master aus Deutschland

we drink you at evening and morning we drink and we drink
this Death is ein Meister aus Deutschland his eye it is blue
he shoots you with shot made of lead shoots you level and
   true
a man lives in the house your goldenes Haar Margarete
he looses his hounds on us grants us a grave in the air
he plays with his vipers and daydreams der Tod ist ein
Meister aus Deutschland

dein goldenes Haar Margarete
dein aschenes Haar Shulamith

translated from the German by John Felstiner

This text, to my mind, is one of the greatest translations of the 20th century. But the word "translation" is misleading. This text does not serve as a mirror. While one appreciates Felstiner's haunting use of German words interspersed with English, readers also know that this striking and powerful juxtaposition of languages (which also occurs in Jerome Rothenberg's earlier translation, as Felstiner has acknowledged) does not occur in Celan's original poem in German.

And yet the English version here is only made more striking as we learn the tragic meaning of the foreign words without needing to know German ourselves—it gives English readers the experience of being *other*, alienated, from language, from power. To realize this is to see clearly that a successful translation, even a "faithful" one, has no need to hold up the mirror to the original. Ultimately it is the poet's process, writes Eavan Boland, that needs to be translated.

*

About this book

The book in your hands is not intended to become one of those heavy scholarly tomes that serve as a "proof" of one's position in the literary/academic hierarchy. Rather, this is a collection of various works, directed at, or inspired by, the words of Paul Celan. What we wanted to make was a living anthology, in which authors observe the poet's work, read it deeply, penetrate and discuss it, but also play with it, remake it, and attempt to fit it into their own worldviews. For what other evidence is there of a poet's significance than the incorporation of his lines, rhythms and vocabulary in the works of those who come after? "They have eaten him to little pieces" testifies that his work, in various incarnations, will continue to intensify decades of poetry to come.

10

We decided not to break this collection into various sections (biographical, critical, etc.), and yet it does contain many different perspectives. We begin with personal accounts (Boland, Young) of readers' encounters, over time, with a poet so different from the traditions of their native literatures and proceed with close readings of the text (Carson, Stewart, Perloff) as well as personal recollections of (Corman, Young, Rothenberg, Daivie). In one way or another, all the responses gathered here are close readings. They include creative responses (a play by Sawako Nakayasu, a lyric by Jean Valentine); philosophical responses (Derrida, Levinas); and even responses to responses (Perloff's response to *Shibboleth*). There are lyrics written towards Celan's style (Forché, Hirsch, Steger, Joris, Howe) and an elegy personally addressing the poet (Amichai). There are comparative studies and reflections (Carson on Simonides, Joron on Goll, Felstiner on Beckett, Robinson on Niedecker, Eshleman on Vallejo). There is also found poetry, alongside poems that retrace Celan's own verse forms (Corey, Hirsch, Bar-Nadav). We include some of the 20th century's most beautiful minds—Jabes, Darwish, Aygi, Derrida, Levinas, Amichai—as well as many of America's finest poets, translators, and critics.

If there is a country named Celania, this book maps only a small part of it, yet we hope it gives a more or less representative view of its longitudes.

Ilya Kaminsky
San Diego, California

11

PAUL CELAN: TRANSLATING THE POET

Eavan Boland

I

I came to Paul Celan late. I knew his name when I was young. I knew something of his work. But I had little enough understanding of what he achieved, or what that achievement meant. I had even less understanding of what he suffered, and what he changed. That huge, blind post-war weight, comprised of a nexus between evil and language was his to shift. And he shifted it.

And yet when I was a young poet, struggling in an intense national culture, finding my way through the Irish story, his work and life seemed somehow remote. I doubt I was unusual in this. In an exchange with James K. Lyon in the seventies, Donald Hall is quoted as saying that by that time "every American poet knew Celan." But this was by no means true of the poets I knew in Ireland. Only a few mentioned him. Hardly anyone I knew seemed to have read his work closely.

There were reasons for this. In describing them, I will try to outline the flaws and uncertainties of the translation process itself. Not simply how a word or line in one language is freighted into another, which is what we usually understand by the term. But the fragile and tenuous process by which one poet finds another. In that sense, this piece is not simply about Celan, and the powerful and poignant journey he made towards meaning. It is also about the strange and uncertain journey meaning itself has to make, from language to language, from poet to poet.

To this day, I see it as part of Celan's power that I found him against the odds. Neither my reading, nor my culture, nor my expectation of what a poet could be, prepared me to find him. But I found him all the same. Not by a scholarly route, nor even a particularly intellectual one. In fact, I often had to consider him in entirely subjective terms if I was to understand him at all.

Even a subjective understanding was missing to begin with. In my twenties I was reading a different sort of male poet: the post-imperial Larkin and the deeply national Lowell. These were writers of landscape and location. After all, I came from a country where the language that pointed at land and identity was causal, not casual. When I read, in Ted Hughes's poem "Pike," a line that described the stillness of the fish as being "as deep as England," I thought I knew what it meant. The poignant phrase seemed to suggest that even nature could be better framed if it was national; that even the universal could be more legible if it was local.

Celan was different. So different as to be almost opposite. By that time I was aware of some of his work, and aware too of the British poet Geoffrey Hill's reverent gestures towards him in his first book, *For the Unfallen*. That reverence was evident in the poem "September Song," about a deportation. The tightly woven stanzas, and the airless grief seemed to be a cryptic homage.

> *As estimated, you died. Things marched,*
> *sufficient, to that end.*
> *Just so much Zyklon and leather, patented*
> *terror, so many routine cries.*

It may well be right there, in someone's advocacy of that poem—

because Hill had admirers in Irish poetry—that I first heard Celan's name. But the name did me little good. When I thought of him at all, I thought of him as opposite everything I relished in the local and national and literary. To my mind he was a tenant of those cold, stellar European spaces of language and expression where everything had broken down. Nation, language, loyalty and even art. Where all aesthetics were subsumed by an ethical code, both arduous and pessimistic. "Try again. Fail again. Fail better," wrote Beckett. Celan seemed of that tribe. I could admire it, but I was not about to seek it out. Occasionally I saw a translation. Occasionally I found his name in an anthology. Sometimes I remembered a line, or a gesture. Then I forgot it again.

I might have remembered more and understood more if I had known then these words by Celan, written by him about the Russian poet, Osip Mandelstam. "The place of the poem remains a human place," he remarked, "'a place in the cosmos,' certainly but here, down here, in time; the poem, with all its horizons, remains a sublunar, a terrestrial, a creaturely phenomenon." And there is also this: "In 1922, five years after the October revolution, *Tristia*, Mandelstam's second volume of poems, comes out. The poet—the man for whom language is everything, origin and fate—is in exile with his language, 'among the Scythians.'"

Celan's words on Mandelstam open out into something I missed and kept on missing. With his insistence on the earthly life of the poet, Celan shucks off that icy shadow I ascribed to him. He comes into the light of engagement and judgment. But there is more to it than that. His comments on Mandelstam suggest something else. They confirm my suspicion of why we are slow to understand certain poets. And they raise a more general concern: not just one poet's delay in understanding an essential poet, but also—more importantly—the tenuous, unreliable ways in which one poet becomes available to another. And since this additional piece of information is central both to the way I missed, and the way I found Celan—and may be representative of other versions of the process—I will try to be clearer about it.

Like many poets in my generation, I was a direct beneficiary of poetic translation. And during the nineteen seventies it was at its height. Ambitious, questing poets were traveling to other languages, encountering the news of other cultures and different outlooks. At the start of the Sixties, for instance, James Wright and Robert Bly brought out their translations of Trakl. And in 1962, the recklessness and energy of Robert Lowell's book *Imitations*, threw out a new paradigm for voicing the work of other poetries.

At first I was a provincial, absolutely unaware of anything but Irish poetry. But gradually, the small patterned volumes of European poets, most published in London, began to find their way into our house. In that way, I sleep-walked into Montale and Akhmatova, Holub and Tsvetayeva, Lorca and Sachs.

But for me, even though I read those books eagerly, there was still something missing. I stood willingly in the cold snows of Pasternak's Peredelkino. I waited in the prison line with Akhmatova. I entered the Hitlerian spring of Montale. I appreciated the craft, the industry with which a poem was freighted from one language to another. And yet when I put the book down that elusive thing was still absent. The language, the texture, the image were there; but not the process. Gradually, I formulated something of my own unease, putting it into my own words. The poem had been translated, I told myself. But no one had translated the poet.

Which brings me to Celan. His poems, once I began to read them, were difficult to understand. I could see they were deeply felt, powerfully intended—that much I understood. But the poet that went with those poems—the vivid, tragic writer, condemned to history and liberated by language—was not yet visible to me. I knew that both poem and poet had to be available if either was to be understood. Something about Celan's own graceful and wrenching comments about Mandelstam suggest that he also realized the poet must be translated as well as the poem. When he describes Mandelstam as "among the Scythians," he is not simply relegating him to a project of language. He is also assigning him to a task of understanding.

II

What does it mean to translate a poet? How does it differ from translating a poem?

Those questions were familiar to me when I began to read Celan more closely. As a young woman I had come across a group of poets who seemed—much like Celan—to be both essential and out of reach. These were the Irish-speaking poets of the 18th century. I knew of their existence. I could trace their presence, their music, their scourging and tragic example all the way to Yeats. But I had gone to school for some years outside Ireland and so I knew no Irish. I felt estranged from their dark witness, but I also knew that as an Irish poet I needed to approach it.

These poets were Irish bards, emerging at the end of a harsh century and on the wrong side of history. For them, a living vision was trapped in a dying language. Even their names—Aodhagan O Rathaille, Eoghan Rua O'Suilleabhain—are redolent of their existence inside the fastness of Gaelic Ireland. They wrote their wounded, barbaric yawps at the cliff edge of that century. In O'Rathaille's case, literally so: He came from the small Kerry townland of Slieve Luachra and, in one of his poems, describes lying on a cliff top on a bitter night, listening to the Atlantic and lamenting the decline of the Gaelic order.

I knew the poems of these poets. They had been amply and eloquently translated. But it was only when the Irish scholar Daniel Corkery tried to translate the poets as well as the poems that I began to understand their meaning. In a powerful passage he wrote:

> We must remember that these poets were simple men, living as peasants in rural surroundings; some of them, probably, never saw a city; not only this, but they were all poor men, very often sore-troubled where and how to find shelter, clothing, food, at the end of a day's tramping. Their native culture is ancient, harking back to pre-Renaissance standards; but there is no inflow of books from outside to impregnate it with new thoughts. Their language is dying: around them is the drip, drip of callous decay: famine overtakes famine, or the people are cleared from the land to make room for bullocks. The rocks in hidden mountain clefts are the only altars left to them; and teaching is a felony.
>
> Not to excuse, but to explain them, are these facts mentioned; for their poetry, though doubtless the poorest chapter in the book of Irish literature, is in itself no poor thing that needs excuse: it is, contrariwise, a rich thing, a

17

marvelous inheritance, bright with music, flushed with color, deep with human feeling. To see it against the dark world that threw it up is to be astonished, if not dazzled.

From then on, I thought translating the poet to be as important as translating his or her poems; and that one without the other was incomplete. But who could translate Celan? Who could convey this complicated poet, together with his poems? How could it be done? Even the thought of it seemed outside my reach. When I weighed the cultural differences between the world I knew and the one he recorded, they seemed weighted towards misunderstanding. The differences were enormous. Just to start with, Ireland had been neutral in the terrible war through which Celan suffered. This was a cultural fact. But there were formal ones as well. The Irish poem was musical and expansive more than it was lyrical and cryptic. The Irish imagination, for all its experience with colony, was often resilient in the face of events. It was hard for me to see how I could access this poet through an Irish experience which had shaped my poetic journey and yet was so remote from his.

When John Felstiner's luminous biography *Paul Celan: Poet, Survivor, Jew* was published, I found elements of this translation. But I also knew that the task could not be assigned to an external reading, even one as fine as Felstiner's. Translating the poet had to be an individual commitment. It had to be an undertaking of decision and selection, just as translating a poem would be. The process, after all is deeply subjective. It draws the poet you are seeking into the ordinary details of your own life. And it was neither precise, nor exact: no scholar would countenance it; and yet any reader might benefit from it.

And so I searched, in seeking out this mysterious and profound figure, for the small signs in my own experience and culture that might reach out to his. And yet how, a critic might ask, can anyone justify seeking out a great witness with small and apparently mundane detail? The question may itself be a category error. Celan's story has a reach and power that is open—as all great stories are—to subjective affinity, and may well be clarified by it.

Take the year 1958 for instance. In Ireland it was a time of stasis. The Republic, founded in 1948—after being a Commonwealth state since 1921—gazed stubbornly inward. Everything that occurred, however contradictory, seemed self-aware and insular. Work began on restoring the staterooms in Dublin Castle. As a grotesque contrast, the Carlisle monument was blown up by political activists in Phoenix Park. Brendan Behan's lovely, wry book *The Borstal Boy* was published and immediately banned by the Censorship Board. Eamon de Valera, the Taoiseach, attended the four-hour coronation of John XXIII in the Vatican.

Violence. Suppression. Reverence. Looking back now, many of the troubles that occurred later in Ireland can all be found in that year, coded into events and customs which appeared routine at the time. The shattering civil uproar in the North and the ominous link between state and Church were all there, waiting to disfigure the future, if we had only known.

1958 began very differently for Paul Celan. In late January he spent a week in Germany. The Hanseatic port city of Bremen, on the northwestern coast, was his destination. He was there to receive the prestigious Literatur-Preises, given annually. "To me this news counts as among the finest that has ever reached me," he wrote back when he was informed of the award. There is something extraordinarily poignant about this poet traveling in this realm of shadows, returning to a country which had generated the death of his parents, but which was also the author-land of the language in which he found both past and future. The themes of language, history, and intent intersect here.

It was this journey, when I read about it first, that began to make Celan plain. I came, after all, from a country where sporadic violence was common; where old hatreds were formative. Where, after the Civil War of 1921—in which close comrades, friends, and even family members had killed each other in the Irish cause—it was said that silence was the only outcome. Men sat across dinner tables from other men. They sat on County Councils. The faced each other in the Dáil. They inhabited the same small rooms of decision and retrospect. But most never mentioned or tried to resolve the terrible past.

The firing squad, the intimate treachery, the ambush, the fire of ideology—they vanished into silence. And so the past lost a language, and my generation a mode of reflection. And I, as a young poet, hearing about such things in anecdotes from my parents, never thought that it could be any different. Silence, it seemed, was a custom of the country. What could language do in the face of what had already happened?

Celan showed what it could do. In one of the 20th century's most important speeches on language and poetry, he addressed the audience at Bremen. Behind him, inviting silence, lay a far more desolate terrain than any Irish conflict had caused, and a more destructive one than any Irish folk memory could imagine. And yet

Celan chose to be there—had eagerly accepted the invitation to be there—to break the silence, not confirm it.

There is a photograph of him at Bremen. He is standing beside Rudolf Alexander Schroder, the Bremen poet. No contrast could be greater. Schroder, a native of the city, a traditional poet, a founder of the periodical *Insel*, stands smiling beside the displaced and questing Celan. In the grainy monochrome the ironies are smoothed away, but not made invisible.

The Bremen speech begins with a courteous meditation on the braiding of words: "Thinking and thanking in our language," he says, "are words from one and the same source. Whoever follows out their meanings enters the semantic field of 'recollect' 'bear in mind' 'remembrance' 'devotion.' Permit me from this standpoint, to thank you."

Adding that he writes poems "to sketch reality for myself," Celan then goes on to comment on language itself, its survival through the darkest ordeal. In John Felstiner's vivid translation the passage reads, "Reachable, near and not lost, there remained in the midst of the losses this one thing: language. It, the language, remained, not lost, yes in spite of everything. But it had to pass through its own answerlessness, pass through frightful muting, pass through the thousand darknesses of deathbringing speech. It passed through and gave back no words for that which happened; yet it passed through this happening. Passed through and could come to light again, 'enriched' by all this."

The translation provides infinite power, but it is especially illuminating to go back to the German text—to see the huge syllabic boulders Celan throws at his listeners. *Antwortlosigkeiten* for "answerlessness." For the line about the thousand darknesses: *die tausend Finsternisse todbringender Rede.* The original words on the page allow the reader to come that bit closer to the irony and force of this event: in the language which caused so much destruction, a great poet commends the survival of the instrument itself.

In these past years I have come to know Celan's work more. Not just the surprising, passionate "Todesfuge" but the mysterious "Mandorla" and the powerful "Psalm." These and other poems are for me, as for so many others, benchmarks of modern poetry: a standard of what the poem can achieve with sound at the very moment it reaches for silence.

But it is the Bremen speech which translated the poet for me even more than these poems. It is that compound of statement and vision which made clear Celan's poetic witness. I could take his words and imagine their effect in other situations—imagine what such an insistence on the truth of language and its survival might have accomplished in my own country. Had those words filtered down, what silences might have been broken, what deceptions might have been prevented.

This is not a logical or exact thought. It may not even be a sustainable one. Celan was a poet, speaking only for himself; and he was speaking in the specific circumstances of his own life and about his own history. As Adorno said, Celan was essentially a hermetic poet. Nevertheless his words in Bremen break through hermeticism and refuse its confinement. For me, they translated the poet he was with remarkable accuracy. If this seems too subjective a reaction, I can invoke Celan's own words about Mandelstam—that the poem remains "a terrestrial, a creaturely phenomenon." For that very reason, there are times when the only way we can apprehend that poem is through the creature who made it. And through the earth he inhabited.

FALSE SAIL

Anne Carson

Humans value economy. Why? Whether we are commending
a mathematician for her proof or a draughtsman for his use of line or
a poet for furnishing us with nuggets of beauty and truth, economy is
a trope of intellectual, aesthetic and moral value. How do we come
to take comfort in this notion? It is arguable that the trope does not
predate the invention of coinage. And certainly in a civilization so
unconditionally committed to greed as ours is, no one questions any
more the wisdom of saving money. But money is just a mediator for
our greed. What does it mean to save time, or trouble, or face, or
breath, or shoe leather? Or words? His biographers recount that when
the poet Paul Celan was four years old, he took a notion to make
up his own fairy tales. He went about telling these new versions
to everyone in the house until his father advised him to cut it out.
"If you need stories the Old Testament is full of them." To make
up new stories, Celan's father thought, is a waste of words.[1] This
father's sentiments are not unusual. My own father was inclined to
make skeptical comments when he saw me hunched at the kitchen
table covering pages with small print. Perhaps poets are ones who
waste what their fathers would save. But the question remains, What
exactly is lost to us when words are wasted? And where is the human
store to which such goods are gathered?

There is a poem of Paul Celan that seems to be concerned with
the gathering in of certain poetic goods to a store that he calls "you."
Among these goods are the lyric traditions of the poetry of courtly
love, of Christian mysticism, of Mallarmé, of Hölderlin, not to say
Celan himself. Celan has chosen to contemplate these traditions
through the focusing device of one brilliant and drastic moment from

---

1   Chalfen (1991), 41.

the romance of Tristan and Isolt: the moment of the false sail.[2]

Matière de bretagne

Ginsterlicht, gelb, die Hänge
eitern gen Himmel, der Dorn
wirbt um die Wunde, es läutet
darin, es ist Abend, das Nichts
rollt seine Meere zur Andacht,
das Blutsegel hält auf dich zu.

Trocken, verlandet
das Bett hinter dir, verschilft
seine Stunde, oben,
beim Stern, die milchigen
Priele schwatzen im Schlamm, Steindattel,
unten, gebuscht, klafft ins Gebläu, eine Staude
Vergänglichkeit, schön,
grüßt dein Gedächtnis.

(Kanntet ihr mich,
Hände? Ich ging
den gegabelten Weg, den ihr wiest, mein Mund
spie seinen Schotter, ich ging, meine Zeit,
wandernde Wächte, warf ihren Schatten—kanntet ihr mich?)

Hände, die dorn-
umworbene Wunde, es läutet,
Hände, das Nichts, seine Meere,

---

2   Celan (1983), 1:171.

Hände, im Ginsterlicht, das
Blutsegel
hält auf dieh zu.

Du
du lehrst
du lehrst deine Hände
du lehrst deine Hände du lehrst
du lehrst deine Hände
              schlafen

[Matière de bretagne

Gorselight, yellow, the slopes
suppurate to heaven, the thorn
pays court to the wound, there is ringing
inside, it is evening, the nothing
rolls its seas toward devotion,
the bloodsail is heading for you.

Dry, run aground
is the bed behind you, caught in rushes
is its hour, above,
with the star, the milky
tideways jabber in mud, stonedate,
below, bunched up, gapes into blueness, a bush-worth
of transience, beautiful,
greets your memory.

(Did you know me,

hands? I went
the forked way you showed, my mouth
spat its gravel, I went, my time,
wandering watches, threw its shadow—did you know me?)

Hands, the thorn-
courted wound, there is ringing,
hands, the nothing, its seas,
hands, in the gorselight, the
bloodsail
is heading for you.

You
you teach
you teach your hands
you teach your hands you teach
you teach your hands
                    to sleep]

What is "gorselight"? Yellow broom flowers. To another poet
they might be beautiful, for Celan they suppurate. Their phrasing
recalls the first verse of Hölderlin's poem "Hälfte des Lebens" ("Half
of Life"): compare the sound of *Ginsterlicht, gelb, die Hänge* and
Mit gelben Birnen hänget.[3] But whereas Hölderlin's yellow pears are
steeped in beauty, Celan's gorse issues pus. The contrast suggests
a mood. The mood continues quietly in Celan's imagery of thorn
and wound, as Christian and courtly conventions of love combine
toward "devotion" (*Andacht*). But what sails toward devotion is "the
Nothing" *(das Nichts)* and the mood swerves into negative theology.

---

3   This connection was suggested by Stanley Corngold, whose conversation with
me about Celan's poem made this essay possible.

As any reader of Celan knows, he is at home in this mood. Here, however, it may be meant to evoke that other "poet of nothingness" whose verse is full of seas and sailing, Mallarmé.[4] Remember the tenth double-page of *Un Coup de dés*, which begins with the word *RIEN* high on the left-hand side and is typeset so that the rest of the words roll themselves out across the page in waves to end in "the wave in which all reality dissolves" at the lower right.[5] Finally, Celan's sea is also a sea of romance bringing Isolt to Tristan on a ship that flies a "bloodsail."

All these fluent traditions run aground in the second stanza, which is dry, stuck on land, lodged in rushes, bushed up, jabbering mud and which engenders the third stanza: five verses stalled in a bracket. The poet's thought stops on itself. His path is forked and his utterance gravel. Celan has crafted these middle verses out of immobility to emphasize the movement of the rest. Seas and phenomena flow again in the fourth stanza and go rolling out the end of the page without a stop. The poem as a whole, recapitulating the first stanza, has the rhythm of a bloodsail, sailing forward in waves from gorselight to gorselight to you.

Celan's "you" is hard to fix, as his bloodsail is a difficult color. If he means a reference to the Tristan legend, the sail should be either white or black. Tristan had arranged this signal with the helmsman bringing Isolt to him by sea: a white sail for Isolt prospering, a black sail for her catastrophe. When Tristan's jealous wife reports to him that the sail is "blacker than a mulberry," Tristan turns his face to

---

4   The label is Sartre's, who also cites George Poulet: "From the outset Mallarmé's poetry is like a mirage…in which he recognized himself not by where or how he is but by where he is not and how he is not." Sartre (1988), 112.

5   Mallarmé (1977), 290–191. There are not a few echoes of Mallarmé throughout the poem, especially in the ringing (cf. Mallarmé's "Le Sonneur") and the blueness (cf. "L'Azur"), not to say the arranged white space into which all disappears at the end.

the wall and dies.[6] There is blood in the old French version but only dreamblood; as Tristan lies dying, Isolt out at sea recalls dreaming that she held in her lap the head of a boar that was staining her all over with its blood and making her robe red.

Blood of course might signify simply fatality. Sail that kills. But let us consider the matter historically. Our oldest literary example of the trope of the false sail comes from the ancient Greek poet Simonides (556–467 B.C.). Simonides mentions the sail and calls it red: φοινίκεον. Indeed he mentions it *in order to call it red*, in defiance of an existing tradition. For the false sail was already an old story by Simonides' time, part of the myth of Theseus, of which other versions existed. Simonides did not scruple to waste a few more words on the subject. The poem he composed is not extant, but we do have two fragmentary citations. From Plutarch we get news of the sail:

> Then Theseus cheered his father by boasting that he would defeat the Minotaur. So his father gave the helmsman a second sail, white this time, telling him to hoist the white sail if he were returning with Theseus safe, otherwise to sail with the black and so signify catastrophe. But Simonides says that the sail given by Aigeus was "not white but a red sail (φοινίκεον ἱστίον) dyed with the wet flower of the blooming holm-oak" and that this was to be the sign of their salvation.[7]

And from a scholiast we have the words of the messenger sent by

---

6   Does the wife lie or is the ship flying the wrong sail? Throughout the old French *version commune* (which, I assume from the title of his poem, is the one Celan has in mind), this point remains unresolved. Spector (1973), 85.

7   Plutarch *Life of Theseus* 17.4; Simonides fr. 550 *PMG*.

Theseus to his father on the day of his return. For according to legend, Theseus is sailing into harbor when he realizes that he forgot to hoist the white sail. A messenger is dispatched to bring the true story to the father, but Aigeus has already read the death-sail and accepted its version. He throws himself into the sea. The messenger is addressing the father's corpse when he says:

> βιότου κέ σε μᾶλλον ὄνασα πρότερος ἐέξλθών.
> [I would have given you a profit greater than life had I come sooner.][8]

Simonides' messenger states his case as economically as possible. His verb (ὄνασα, from ὀνίνημι "to profit") is drawn from the sphere of commercial gain. More important, his statement takes the form of a contrary-to-fact condition. Why must the economy of the false sail be contrafactual? Because it is an impossible idea conditioned by the negative event that already exists. Two realities for the price of one. No profit in fact changes hands—but the idea of it, added to the account contrafactually, multiplies pathos and learning. Aigeus' salvation is both adduced and canceled in the messenger's spare comment. You could have your sail and falsify it too, if words were true.

White, black, red, telling, lying, lied about, forgotten, fatal, all in all the falsity of the false sail is a rich proposition. How such propositions extend themselves to form the interior of a poem like "Matière de Bretagne" is hard to say. Celan combines the local Bretagne stuff of courtly traditions and ancient sailing with the local Bretagne stuff of gravel, hours, beds and personal pronouns that fold over one another like hands. He transcribes a circle of great lyrical

---

8   Scholiast *ad* Sophokles *Ajax* 740; Simonides fr. 551 *PMG*.

beauty, lit by gorselight, around Nothingness. *Das Nichts* occurs twice but this word does not stop the poem or spoil the light. It is simply part of the poet's *matière*. So too Simonides constructs the truth about the false sail negatively. "Not white but red," he insists and then goes on to matters of local color: "dyed with the wet flower of the blooming holm-oak." The redness of his red sail stains fact deeply with the fixative of counterfact. Redder than red, redder than the blood of a boar in a dream, is the φοινίκεον that rests on white nothing.

Negation links the mentalities of Simonides and Celan. Words for "no," "not," "never," "nowhere," "nobody," "nothing" dominate their poems and create bottomless places for reading. Not white but red. Was it not Aristotle who said, "A mistake enriches the mere truth once you see it as that." Both Simonides and Celan are poets who see it as that. And ask us to see it as that. Us in the gorselight.

That is why the whole of Celan's poem gathers us into a movement—toward you—that sails to the end. But you, by the time we reach you, are just folding yourself away into a place we cannot go: sleep. Blank spaces instead of words fill out the verses around you as if to suggest your gradual recession down and away from our grasp. What could your hands teach us if you had not vanished? To stand at this border with whiteness exhausts our power of listening and makes us aware of a crisis in you. We travel toward your crisis, we arrive, yet we cannot construe it—the terrible thing is, after all (and most economically!) we are the false sail for which you wait.

Author's note: Fragments of Simonides are cited from the editions of Page (1962) = *PMG*; Page (1981) = *FGE*; and West (1971) = *W*. All translations are my own unless otherwise noted.

FOR A LONG TIME:
INTO WHISPERINGS AND RUSTLINGS

Gennady Aygi

> *Once more—in memory of Paul Celan*

Whisperings, rustlings. As if wind were penetrating into a cold storeroom and flour scattering somewhere. Or—straw trembling in a yard abandoned by all. The rustling is the coming into being of some land.

    "To be a mouse," said *that poet.*[1] To be a mouse. Vertiginous. Ripples. Afterward they said it was poison. Half-a-Pole. Ha-alf....As if behind the whispering of clothes was a cut. From the slaughterhouse. And hidden in the rustling—blood. Even if it was only man-clothing. Alone, alone,—with the liquids of torture.

    But reb-be, made of all things—of *this* and of *that*—you were so much one,—dirt, a torn book, and blood,—oh almost Transparency,—winter dance in the street, tattered jacket, man-snowdrifts (for everywhere was the sweat of poverty,—even in straw: there—in the wind, and the scattered handful of flour).

    Life, rebbe.

    And then,—here. This face . . .—all-embracing. It is as if you are walking through the city, and everywhere it is "mine," every corner of it. Vertiginous. Then—the ripples. And even if it was only: a garden (all this is face, in the face) splashed out there—inaccesssibly. It sprang back, pain—as from glass. And—*you cannot squeeze in.* "A garden—just a garden." Like a popular tune. Bottomless. And—close at hand.

    And how does it happen in the voice—some bottom lies concealed. And do we converse in words? Wind. Bottomless. You

---

1   Aleksander Wat.

cannot name it—even with signs.

And this man from Hungary.[2] Simply—a fraternal grave, no more. They dug him out—*with all the others* (and this is what matters most) into the light of Day, and suddenly—there was the Motherland. The question solved. *With all the others* (this matters most).

"God"—not the right expression. There is only: "And God?" For ever and ever.

And then—those journeys. Rol-ling stone. For prizes. And speeches. All correct. In honor of. And all—seems: floating-in-air! And as if through heaven it wan-ders: pain-language,—alone,—for heaven. All empty. Give up the ghost,—huddle up,—only pain. Language?—the Wind of the Universe.

Oh how simple it is. This "simple," there is no place for it in language. (You can try. Straight out will come—a thing. "The simple,"—such Freedom—compare it: the mind brought collapse.)

Ripples. Simple, vertiginous.

Oh, whisperings, my clothing. Straw. T-r-a-sh. Oh, rustling, my skin. I-motherland, I such-clothing-and-flesh. With whispering-skin.

Ripples.

But no one cries out. That-is. Not I then. "I" is sticky. There is something other (behind—the whispering. Behind this rustling).

And in the water walks the sight of this Frenchman. Car-r-ion. What is this,—the essence?—the clothing? The one-ness.

Forget. Oh, when then. Forget. And—p u r i t y b e g i n s. And.

Ripples. With all the dirt—of torture.

No floating back up.

---

2   Miklós Radnóti.

No-*Baptême.*
No-o.

translated from the Russian by Peter France

A CLOUD FROM SODOM

Mahmoud Darwish

After your night, night of the last winter,
the sea road turned empty of its night guards,
and no shadow follows me after your night dried up
in my song's sun. Who will say to me
now: Let go of yesterday and dream with all
of your subconscious?
My freedom sits beside me, with me, and on
my knees like a house cat. It stares at me and at
what you might have left of yesterday for me: your lilac
shawl, videotapes of dancing among wolves, and a jasmine
necklace around the algae of the heart . . .

What will my freedom do, after your night,
night of the last winter?
"A cloud went from Sodom to Babylon,"
hundreds of years ago, but its poet Paul
Celan committed suicide, today, in Paris's river.
You won't take me to the river again. No guard
will ask me: What's your name today? We won't curse
war. We won't curse peace. We won't climb
the garden fence searching the night for two willows
and two windows, and you won't ask me: When
will peace open our citadel doors to the doves?

After your night, night of the last winter,
the soldiers pitched their camp in a faraway place
and a white moon alighted on my balcony

as I sat with my freedom silently staring into our night:
Who am I? Who am I after your night
night of the last winter?

translated from the Arabic by Fady Joudah

CELAN'S BREAKTHROUGH BOOK*

David Young

I was unusually fortunate in being able to meet and talk to Paul Celan in the summer of 1966. Stuart Friebert and I had been traveling on a grant to interview contemporary German poets for an anthology we were contemplating. Our last scheduled stop was with Celan, in Paris. "He'll never see you," the other poets told us. It was clear that they all thought he was very difficult, and also clear that they all considered him a key figure, perhaps the most important poet among them.

The man we met, along with his wife, the artist Gisèle Lestrange, was in fact cordial, even courtly, and, while clearly somewhat reserved and formal, very willing to discuss his poems. We talked in their apartment and they presented us with one of her prints, with signed copies of two of his books, and with a limited edition fine press book they had produced together, *Atemkristall*, made up of her etchings and his poems. They were interested in the possibility of a show of her work in the United States. Indeed, he seemed more interested in promoting her art than his own. I found him self-possessed and, while outwardly modest, a poet who was confident and centered, clearly well aware of his own worth and importance.

At the time, though, it seemed to me that Celan's poems were just too difficult, and arbitrarily so. Other poets we'd met—Günter Eich, Karl Krolow, Helmut Heisenbüttel, Günter Grass, Hilde Domin, Rainer Brambach—interested me more, and I was drawn to the challenge of translating them. Celan seemed to me to resist both translation and interpretation. Part of this was just my own

---

* Adapted from the introduction to David Young's translation of *From Threshold to Threshold* (Marick Press, 2010).

inexperience (I was in my late twenties): the poem "Assisi," for example, was difficult for me partly because I simply didn't know enough about Saint Francis at that time. But in general the world of Celan's poems seemed unfriendly and private—a barren realm of ice, rock, staring eyes, and frosty stars. I knew, of course, about his history as a Holocaust survivor, and admired, as did everybody else, his famous poem "Todesfuge"; but while I found the man approachable, his poems seemed the opposite, and I read him very little for a great many years thereafter.

Four years after our meeting Celan drowned himself in the Seine. Clearly there were problems and abysses in the man that we had little inkling of from our meeting. Meanwhile, although interest in his work grew steadily, good translations were hard to come by. I heard from someone that Celan had designated Joachim Neugroschel as his exclusive American translator, cutting out the gifted Cid Corman, who had been doing versions of his poems for some time. Michael Hamburger, in England, was producing versions of Celan poems that were treated respectfully because Hamburger was, after all, the eminent German translator of his generation. When it appeared, the *Neugroschel* volume (1971) did not fare well with reviewers, and Hamburger's efforts (1972), I would say, produced respect without much accompanying enthusiasm. So Celan remained at a distance to most of us while his reputation as a major figure in poetry for the second half of the twentieth century grew steadily.

*

In recent years, the translation situation has much improved, as the Celan estate has relaxed exclusivity and a variety of translators have stepped bravely forward: John Felstiner, Pierre Joris, Muska Nagel, Katherine Washburn and Margaret Guillemin, Heather

McHugh and Nikolai Popov, Ian Fairley, Walter Billeter, Brian Lynch and Peter Jankowsky, Rosemarie Waldrop (Celan's prose)... my list is probably incomplete. Much more of Celan is available to us now, often in multiple versions, which are certainly helpful in allowing readers to try and *surround* these difficult poems as a way of understanding them more fully. Hamburger in Britain, and Joris and Felstiner in America, have been industrious in keeping up the pace, while Celan scholars, by exegesis and research, have opened up this poet's canon more and more fully. In the forty-two years since I met him, Celan's place has become secure, among all readers with a serious interest in the art of poetry, and his availability in English is much richer and more varied.

For my own part, during the summer of 2004 I decided to try and come to terms with a poet whom I had avoided for so long, as we were preparing a *FIELD* symposium on his work. Translating is, for me, always the most thoroughgoing form of reading, and so I set myself to the task of translating through his second volume, *Von Schwelle zu Schwelle* (1955). This was the book, I felt, in which the Celan we know, admire, and find difficult truly emerged. I wanted to witness that emergence, and, more and more as I worked along, I wanted to understand the volume's organization. If Celan poems are difficult from the outside, sometimes inscrutable as the stones that populate them, one solution that proposes itself is the recognition that they are comfortable in each other's company: they converse with one another, in effect, and their intimacy constitutes a feature in which readers can participate.

I would urge readers first to read *From Threshold to Threshold* straight through, without bothering greatly about interpretation. When they have done that, have fully entered the distinctive world that Celan constructed, they can relax and begin to be at home. Individual poems, revisited, will start to yield their meanings, to feel easier and less opaque. It is a little like reading René Char or Samuel Beckett: what strikes you first is the strangeness; over time, what impresses you is the consistency and what I have called the integrity. These writers are uncompromising, in great part as a response to historical circumstances. And their integrity and consistency is the source of their greatness.

*

When interpretation is difficult and we are looking for quick fixes, we can misread a poet by making too much of any one identifiable feature. In Celan's case it is easy to fix on his Jewishness, on his sense of guilt as a Holocaust survivor (he escaped the death camps while his parents perished there), on his lover's quarrel with the German language (his mother's tongue was her murderers' tongue), on his pessimism about any surviving meaning for God in a post-Holocaust world, on his literary quarrels (he was unjustly accused of plagiarizing the poems of Yvan Goll and Osip Mandelstam, an episode that left him suspicious and anguished), and on his desire to create a completely new poetry. In truth, *all* these issues play over his poems, which is why singling out one and fixing too firmly on it can never do him justice. He is a poet of considerable range, and his interests include geology, history, linguistics, semiotics, philosophy, and astronomy, among others. He is obsessive, but never about just one thing. His aim is to take a corrupted and ruined world, and, reforming a corrupted and compromised language, to start over, striving for the impossible: a reborn world and a renewed language for it. Pessimistic and hopeful at the same time, he proposes to make language, specifically the German language, the instrument of expression and truth that it was in the hands of poets like Hölderlin, and to do this in a world so devastated and drained of meaning that the task before him appears almost unworkable.

He must be extremely open and he must preserve, at all costs, his artistic integrity. The difficulties and exigencies of his life—the hardship of making a living, the encounters with anti-Semitism, the comparative rootlessness of living in postwar France, the absence from his life of kindred spirits and sympathetic readers—all this must be put to one side when he writes. Then and only then can the truth move through him and find its expression in the stripped-down, simplified landscapes and mindscapes of his poems. As long as the poems come, something exists as a barrier between Paul Celan and utter despair; but his time is short and his creative string will eventually run out and leave him helpless. Not before he has produced a body of work that we can and should prize for its uniqueness.

*

Celan's world is one in which distinctions we are used to, between living and dead, between inner and outer, between dreaming and waking, have been dissolved. In that sense it is a visionary's, or mystic's, world. The difference, of course, is that this visionary has no faith in the consistent presence of divinity in his world, doubts the capability of language to express the inexpressible, and is disoriented at the very idea of being a self who can communicate with other selves. Reading this book is a matter of adjusting to that condition, to the tension that Pierre Joris has described as "on the one hand the need to witness, and, on the other...to create in and through the poems a new viable world that would overcome the past—without abolishing or dismissing it." (Joris, *Paul Celan: Selections,* 25). Joris marks this tension as a feature of the later work, but it is useful, I think, to realize that we encounter it as early as this 1955 volume.

Perhaps we can glimpse how it operates, poem to poem, by tracing as a sequence the seven poems that open this book's second section.

The first poem is "Epitaph for François," written for Celan's son, who died in infancy. It is therefore openly personal, to an unusual degree for this poet, and he even dates it, *October 1953* (the only poem he ever dated in this way):

> Both the world's doors
> stand open:
> you opened them
> in this divided night.
> We hear them slam and slam,
> bearing all the uncertainty,
> bearing the Green that is
> into your Ever.

This is an unusual way in which to express parental grief and a sense of the death's meaning. There's a sense of enormous restraint in the presence of powerful emotion. The living are passive listeners. The dead child is the active one, the one who has opened both the world's doors and then, perhaps, slammed them shut again. For the living, the night is "divided" (*Zwienacht*), or a "twinight," a two-night, as two other translators have it, doubly dark with loss. Perhaps that is why they perceive two doors, one from life into death, the other from death into life. But the slamming of the doors (or are they "banging and banging," as Felstiner's version has it?) leaves the living bearing their uncertainty—about the relation of living and dead, about their world, about whether the world's "green" can be translated in an "evergreen" that promises afterlife and immortality. The poem poses questions about death and afterlife, rather than providing answers, and the emotion, while somewhat muffled, emerges strongly once we are oriented to it.

The two poems that follow—"Grafted to Your Eye" and "Whoever Counted the Hours for Us"—continue to sketch out this visionary but problematic world. We no longer have an event, such as the death of the child, to anchor them for us, so our speculations are more open, less certain. The "you" of the first may be the poet, the reader, or someone else. The "we" of the second is similarly open to multiple possibilities.

We are perhaps relieved, then, when we get to "Assisi," to be able to link the poem to a specific place and a specific figure associated with it, Saint Francis. This poem's chant-like form, with its three glimpses—the Umbrian night, the clay vessel, and the trotting animal (perhaps the wolf that Francis is supposed to have tamed, or, as Glenn suggests (80), a donkey associated with humility and poverty)—is intriguing, as are the refrains or responses that seem, in two instances, to provoke the next stanza and at the end to close off the Saint's answers and hopes. We note that the wolf (or donkey) could be meaningful in God's world, a world since shut down so that language cannot contain divinity: "a word that was locked like a door" (Felstiner: "the word that slammed shut," Hamburger, "the word that clicked shut"). Here we have again the image of the world as a house that once had meaning, where there was an interaction between the physical and the metaphysical, and is now robbed of it. Light, even though it is brightness, "gives no comfort" and the dead inhabit a kind of poverty in which they beg the saint for comfort he cannot give. The poem is bleak, beautiful, and more accessible than the two that have preceded it. It continues the metaphysical questioning of the "Epitaph," again without finding any definite answers.

Now comes a poem, "This Evening Too," that seems to sketch out the poet's role as someone who is trying to maintain a habit of exchange—experience for meaning—in a world that is problematically robbed of such possibility. The "you" of this poem, who seems to be a figure for the poet, takes baskets of ice to the city and tries to barter them for sand that will feed his roses (perhaps by making the trickle of time through the hourglass a process of growth that will lead to more roses and more bartering). His world, with its snow on a sea that is also drenched with sunlight, is beautiful but mysterious, and his "marketing" feels constrained by materials—ice and sand—that will surely interfere with its success. And yet the ice and sand are part of nature, which suggests that the rearrangement of meanings the poems have been tracing is not so much a meaningless-ness as a new and dramatically austere order that must be fully acknowledged and embraced.

The next poem, "In Front of a Candle," is one of the longest and most moving in the book. Again, we feel more oriented here because the speaker, addressing his dead mother, performs a ritual in her memory that produces first a "daughter" of her deadness ("your being-dead's daughter," in Felstiner's version) and then a kind of anti-prayer. Felstiner, who is particularly interested in Celan's Jewishness, reads this poem with confidence and tenderness, and I recommend his account of it (*Paul Celan,* 73-74). My own purpose here is to move on to the poem that follows, proposing itself as the title work of the sequence we have been following:

WITH A KEY THAT KEEPS CHANGING

With a key that keeps changing
you unlock the house—inside:
the snowdrifts of what's never spoken.
The key changes in keeping
with the blood that wells up

from eye or mouth or ear.

If your key changes, the word changes,
allowed to drift with the snowflakes. Depending
on the wind that pushes you away,
the snow packs round your word.

My handling of the first line is rather free, as a more literal rendering
would be "with a changing key" (Felstiner) or a "variable key"
(Hamburger and Joris). My sense is that it is uncanny to have a stable
thing, a key meant always to open the same lock, be unstable. And I
like the way "keeps changing" can reappear as "changes in keeping,"
the sort of word-play Celan was given to. In any case, this unstable
key, like the sequence we have been following, signals the poet's
dilemma in this new and problematic world. The house he unlocks
with his transformed and transforming key is already familiar to us
from the doors of the "Epitaph" and the locked word of "Assisi," and
it can be said to represent his memory and his consciousness (Glenn).
The paradox of finding snow *inside* is typical of Celan's dissolving
of inside-outside distinctions, and the snow, as several commentators
have noted, is rightly associated both with his parents' deaths and
with his recent loss of his son, who is François in French, Francisco
(Saint Francis) in Italian, and Franz (e.g. Kafka) in German (the final
rhyme of "Assisi" is "Glanz / Franz"). The bleak world that the poet
finds in his own house, unlocked with his unstable key, is one of
wintry cold and constant change. Change associates it with his blood,
a welling up of emotion and woundedness, and with the dire winter
of the soul, which packs its snow around his word and gives him
little comfort in his creativity. Nor, as Glenn notes (84-85), does he
claim much artistic control: the snow and wind determine his content
and he is their spokesperson and victim all at once.

The poem is bleak but oddly affirmative once we have understood its austerity. And we note that we are able to understand its images—the key, the house, the blood, the word, the snow and wind—in part because we have encountered them elsewhere. This is one illustration of the way that the poems "converse," as I have suggested, and slowly open themselves up to the patient reader/listener by means of their intertextuality.

*

I have argued elsewhere against the danger of reading Celan too allegorically, by which I meant that the ready transference of signifier to signified, e.g. snow = Shoa, oversimplifies this poet's technique (*FIELD,* 19-20). The snow is always snow, and its other associations pack themselves around it, so to speak. It's good to work first on the literal level with Celan, feeling our way forward just as he did, with less assurance and more openness than allegorizing requires. When we work this way we duplicate, to some extent, his creative process, and that, of course, is also what the translator tries to do.

Translation is a humbling art, but it is a particularly humbling experience to attempt translation of this poet. I still worry about whether that key should "keep changing" or just be "variable" (surely weak for the sense it carries here?) or simply "changing." I suspect that the different associations of the German word "wechselndem" and the English words "variable" and "changing" are behind my decision to add something to Celan's austere title and first line. But I am hesitant about such moves and glad that the other versions exist. I have added a rare interpretive gesture to a poem that can never come completely out of its ferocious and problematic existence in German. Nor would we want it to, though translators will naturally dream of a success they always fall short of.

I wish to present one other poem from this collection, mostly as a way of emphasizing its range and variety. This one is more exuberant, less bleak, than most of the others I have discussed, and it shows that while Celan may characterize his creative process as bleakly as in "This Evening Too" and "With a Key That Keeps Changing," he also has moments that are somewhat more festive and playful. Translators have not tended to select this poem, which suggests that a narrower portrait of this artist's range has perhaps emerged from choices for translation based on assumptions about his suffering and his obsession with the deaths of his parents. Those elements are not absent from the poem that follows, but they do not entirely dominate it either:

EVENING OF THE WORDS

Evening of the words—water-diviner in the stillness!
One step and then another,
a third, whose trace
your shadow does not obliterate:

the scar of time
opens
and floods the land with blood –
the mastiffs of the word-night, those mastiffs
are baying now
within you:
they feast the wilder thirst,
the wilder hunger...

One last moon leaps to your aid:
he takes a long silver bone
—naked as the road on which you came—
and throws it to the pack of hounds,
although that doesn't save you:
the beam which you woke
foams toward you
and on top of it swims a fruit
into which you sank your teeth
many years ago.

While this poem contains many of the same reservations about
a changed and problematic world that we have learned to expect
from Celan, I would also note that it presents a view of the creative
process that is both fierce and celebratory. The poet, who is searching
like a water-diviner during language's evening, faces threats in the
form of the mastiffs, that are in fact within him. But the moon, that
traditional sponsor of imagination and change, distracts the dogs with
a bone that is probably moonlight's reflection on water, and while
that doesn't altogether "save" the poet-figure, it allows him to revisit
an experience of tasting fruit that is in some ways quite positive. The
fruit may well be the forbidden fruit which Adam tasted, but that
somehow helps to validate the creative process, its recalling of our
lost paradise.

Other readers may find my account of this poem too positive
and playful, but to me its grim fun lightens some of the bleaker
insights and moods that Celan is famous for, widening his range
and fundamental appeal. Other poems in this collection that I value
for similar reasons include "In the Evening Glow," "You Talk Too,"
and "Argumentum e Silentio," the poem dedicated to René Char. In

general, it can be said that the more affirmative elements of Celan's poems emerge slowly, after we have dealt with the difficult and unpleasant truths.

WORKS CITED

Celan, Paul. *Atemkristalle.* With etchings by Gisèle Celan-Lestrange. Paris: Brunidor, 1965. Our gift copy of this is now in Oberlin's Special Collections.

_____. *Von Schwelle zu Schwelle.* Stuttgart: Deutsche Verlags-Anstalt, 1955.

Felstiner, John. *Paul Celan: Poet, Survivor, Jew.* New Haven: Yale, 1995.

_____. *Selected Poems and Prose of Paul Celan.* New York: Norton, 2001.

Glenn, Jerry. *Paul Celan.* New York: Twayne, 1973.

Hamburger, Michael. *Poems of Paul Celan.* 1972, 1980, 1988. Revised and Expanded Edition. New York: Persea Books, 2002.

Joris, Pierre. *Paul Celan: Selections.* Berkeley: University of California, 2005. See also Joris' translations of the individual late volumes *Breathturn, Threadsuns,* and *Lightduress,* all published by Green Integer, Copenhagen, 2004.

Nagel, Muska, *A Voice . . .* Orono: Puckerbrush Press, 1998.

Neugroschel, Joachim, *Speech-Grille and Selected Poems.* New York: Dutton, 1971.

Popov, Nikolai, and McHugh, Heather. *Glottal Stop: 101 Poems by Paul Celan.* Middletown: Wesleyan U. Press, 2000.

Waldrop, Rosmarie. *Paul Celan: Selected Prose.* New York: Routledge, 2003.

Washburn, Katherine, and Guillemin, Margret. *Paul Celan: Last Poems.* San Francisco: North Point, 1986.

Young, David. "'To Be Written Under a Picture': The Poet as Allegorist and Visionary." *FIELD: Contemporary Poetry and Poetics.* Number 71, Fall, 2004.

I have not listed here additional translations by Ian Fairley, Walter Billeter, and others. Most of them may be found in the Bibliography of Joris' *Selections,* with the exception of Fairley's *Schneepart,* which has just appeared (2007) from Sheep Meadow Press.

NORTHTRUE.
SOUTHBRIGHT

Dan Beachy-Quick

Gong-world—I strike you
            and you
Speak me. Not-golden—

You speak me not-bronze.

Nor am I comet
        myself enough
To hammer through to you my need

Not to be
        a speaking-ear, not
A tongue
        that listens

Woodstar, woodstar—cancel
                out the fuel
You burn in me
            on. I am not
Made-of-you
            who am made
Of burning. I feel the tip-of-flame

And not flame's whole fury.

I'd unpeople me
For you—
Unleaf the tree I'm not—
                (I am)

First forest-out, out
                side the door
The forest
        less wild
                inside
The door made into the door.
I was me, most me, then.

Inforest, inforage, infest, infrost . . .
I know
        another tree grows

A knot into a wood-star—whorled
        grain—

To each word I have not said. I can't

Solve myself outside you
         can I—
         can I

Ask you for a star inside
         that tree

(to threaten wood) I
         would

Promise me again that tree is me.

         unknock

The flame: unlit that wick is yet.

Now who's spark?
         Who tinder and who
               flint?

Leaves more quick than stone—
           and then

The stones are quicker.

Inside the house
         on floor-plank, slat-

forest.

Strong there—I knock

On my door's both sides
            at once—

Double-wilderness—

Wildness is where I cannot let me go.

BEING AND THE OTHER: ON PAUL CELAN

Emmanuel Lévinas

1   Towards the Other

"I see no difference," Paul Celan writes to Hans Bender, "between a handshake and a poem."

Here then is the poem—perfected language—at the level of an interjection, of an expression as little articulated as the blink of an eye or a sign given to one's neighbor! Sign of what? of life? good-will? complicity? Sign either of nothing or of complicity for no reason: to speak without speech. Or a sign which is its own signified: the subject signals that gift of sign to the point of making itself into a sign. An elementary communication, without revelation—mumbling infancy of discourse, awkward entry into the celebrated "speaking of language," the celebrated "*die Sprache spricht*": a beggar's entry into the "dwelling place of Being."

It thus comes about that Paul Celan—whom Heidegger nonetheless saw fit to praise during one of his trips to Germany[1]— tells us of the little understanding he has of a certain language which founds the world in Being and which signifies as the shining forth of pre-Socratic "*physis*." Rather, Celan compares language to a "lovely...incomparable road" in the mountains, where "to the left blooms the turk's-cap lily, blooms wild, blooms as nowhere else, and to the right stands the rhapontic, and diunthus superbus, the superb pink is not far off...a language not for you and not for me—because, I ask you, who is it meant for, the earth, not for you, I tell you, is it meant, and not for me—a language, yes indeed, without any I and without any Thou, nothing but He, nothing but It, do you understand,

---

1   Each of which "altered him profoundly" according to incontestable witness.

53

nothing but She, and that's all." Language of the neuter.

It thus comes about that, for Paul Celan, the poem situates itself precisely at that level which is pre-syntactic and pre-logical (as is currently *de rigeur*)—but which is also prior to "unconcealment": at the moment of pure touch, of pure contact, of that grasping, that pressing which is, perhaps, a way of giving even to the hand that gives. A language of and for proximity—more ancient than that of the "truth of Being" (which it probably bears and supports), the first of languages—response preceding question, responsibility to the neighbor—making possible through its "for the other" the whole miracle of giving.

The poem "continues to make for that 'other,' which it considers to be attainable, capable of being set free, and, perhaps, unoccupied..." Around this proposition from "The Meridian" is built a text wherein Celan delivers what he perceives of his poetic act. An elliptical and allusive text, interrupting itself ceaselessly so as to let its other voice enter into these interruptions, as if two or more discourses were superimposed with a strange coherence which is not that of dialogue, but is rather accorded to a counterpoint which—despite their immediate melodic unity—constitutes the fabric of his poems. But the vibrant formulas of "The Meridian" are nonetheless extremely precise and call for interpretation.

The poem goes toward the other. It hopes to rejoin it, free and unoccupied. The solitary work of the poet carving the precious stuff of words[2] is an act of "ambushing" a "vis-a-vis." The poem "becomes conversation—it is often futile conversation... encounters, a voice's paths to a thou capable of perception"—Are Buber's categories to be preferred then? Are they to be preferred to so much inspired exegesis to the benefit of Hölderlin, Trakl, and

---

2   "Hand work," Celan writes Bender.

Rilke, that descends in majesty from the Black Forest in order to show poetry opening the world in Being, between heaven and earth, where man finds a dwelling place? Are they to be preferred to the aligning of structures in the intersidereal space of Objectivity—the precariousness of which, in Paris, the poet rightly senses, having the good or bad luck to align himself, belonging, with the entirety of his being, to the very objectivity of these structures? Poetics of the avant-garde where the poet has no personal destiny. Buber is without question preferred to them. The poetry of the poem will be the personal: "...the poem does speak! It remains mindful of its dates, but—it speaks, to be sure, it speaks only in its own, its own individual cause." The personal: from me to the other. But the breathless meditation of Celan—daring to cite Malebranche from a text on Kafka by Walter Benjamin, and Pascal according to Leo Schestow—imitates no one. It must be heard more closely.

The poem which was speaking of me, speaks "in the cause of an other"; "a wholly other"; already it speaks with an other, "an 'other' which is not far removed, which is very near"; "it makes for that other"; already "we are outside, at a considerable distance," already "in the light of utopia." "Literature...shoots ahead of us. *La Posie, elle aussi, brûle nos étapes.*"

2   Transcendence

The movement thus described—going from place to nonplace, from *here* to u-topia—is transcendence. That there is, in Celan's essay on poetry, an attempt to think transcendence cannot be doubted.[3]

---

3   To expect from poetry that which is given neither in perception nor in concepts is perhaps—independent of Celan's original path—in the tradition of the discovery of the Kantian problem of the schematism, rather than that of some positivist

"Poetry—this conversion of mortality and futility into the infinite. The paradox of this transcendence lies not in the origin of its adventure starting in futility, but in the contradiction of its very concept: a leap across the abyss open in Being—a leap to which the very identity of the leaper gives the lie. Must we not die to transcend—against nature, against the essence of Being, against logic: or to leap and yet not leap—and in what duration?—unless the I were able to disengage from self? In Celan's terms: discover a "place where a person succeeded in setting himself free, as an— estranged I." Unless the poem which goes to the other—"turned to face him"—were to go and not go; in Celan's terms (which remain ambiguous): "takes its position at the edge of itself." Unless the poem, to endure, holds back its acumen—in Celan's terms: "...

---

exaltation of the concrete and sensible. A characteristic mark of modern rationalism: along side of the mathematisation of fact through an ascent to pure forms, the schematisation of the intelligible through a descent into the sensible. Schematised in the concrete, the formal concepts resonate with new significations. To unfold the categories in time is certainly to limit the rights of reason, but it is also to discover a physics at the very bottom of the logico-mathematical structures: the abstract idea of *substance* becomes the principle of mass-conservation, and that of community, the principle of the interaction of beings. In Hegel do not the figures of the dialectic draw themselves, with particular vigor in figuring the history of humanity? Is not Husserlian phenomenology a way of "schematising" the real in the unsuspected horizons of sensible subjectivity? Just as formal logic is referred by Husserl to the concreteness of subjectivity, so the worlds of perception and history, in their pure objectivity, betray their abstraction and become "guiding threads" for the discovery of those horizons of sense wherein they take on their true signification. In reading the recent and remarkable book on psychoanalysis by Alphonse de Waelhens—a philosopher from whom neither Husserl nor Heidegger have any secrets—we had the impression that Freudianism itself does nothing more than restore the phenomenologically *sensible*—which would still be logical in its images, its contraries, its convergences and repetitions—to a sort of yet more sensible, more "impure" sensibility. Notably, in psychoanalysis the opposition of masculine and feminine makes possible a deeper schematism. (A. de Waelhens: *Psychose*; Nauwelaerts; Paris & Louvain). Our traditional sensibility would thus be as abstract as the principle of causality before the *Critique of Pure Reason*. An entire drama then lies coiled in the "ether" of our most critical concepts.

without interruption calls and fetches itself from its now no-longer back into its as-before." But a place where, in view of this as-before, the poet would not know how to keep, in passing to the other, the sovereignty of self. In Celan's terms: the Poet "speaks from under the angle of inclination of his existence, the angle of inclination of his position among all living creatures....Whoever writes it must remain in its company." Singular desubstantiation of the I! Make oneself sign—or make oneself trace—it is, perhaps, that.[4]

Enough of glorious, creative poses! "Let's not be bothered with *poein* and such nonsense," writes Celan, again to Bender, talking about the production of poems. A sign made to the other, a handshake, a speaking without speech—much more important in its "inclination" than in its message. The "attention as the natural prayer of the soul" of which Malebranche speaks through the pen of Walter Benjamin. Attention—mode of consciousness without distraction— which is to say: without power to evade in its shadowy depths; a full light, not to make knowledge possible, but to forbid escape: that is the original sense of the insomnia that is consciousness. Rightness of the responsibility, above all, to be evident.

Things appear, and images: the speech of this poetic speaking. Things appear at last in the very movement that brings them to the other; personified, but as figures of this movement. "Each thing, each person is a form of the other for the poem, as it makes for this other...that which is addressed take(s) form and gather(s) around the I who is addressing and naming it." In this offering, this giving, forms emerge and take on meaning—the for-other of the *speaking of Man* speaking to the other, and not the *speaking of Being* which evokes a presence blossoming in the landscape to which the

---

4   Simone Weil writes somewhere: "Father, tear from me this body and this soul to make things for yourself, and leave of me only, eternally, that tearing itself." Cited in Vetö: *La Philosophie de Simone Weil*; Vrin; Paris.

poem would respond. The act of the poem speaking to its neighbor precedes all evocation; but it is in poetic speaking outstretched toward the other that, as if by magic, things assemble their qualities as things. The for-other precedes the perception of evidence. The poem thus leaves to the real the alterity which pure imagination erases. Poetry "allow(s) the most idiosyncratic quality of the other, it's time, to participate in the conversation." Do not poetry and art begin—rather than in the cruelties of tragedy—in the for-other speaking to the other precisely this for-other, in signaling this very giving of the sign, in love speaking that love, in lyricism? Song of songs!

Does this departure toward the other person lead to some "outside"? The word "utopia" designates the term to the movement which Celan accords the poem. A step "beyond human nature...yet not devoid of human characteristics"—as if humanity were a species that admitted at the interior of its logical space—its extension—a total rupture; as if, in moving toward the other man, one transcended the human. And as if the utopian were not the lot of some accursed wandering, but rather the clearing in which man shows himself: "... in light of u-topia....And human beings? And all living creatures?...In this light."

3   In Light of Utopia

This exceptional "outside" is not an other landscape. Beyond the simply strange in art—and beyond the opening of the Being of beings[5]—the poem takes a further step: the strange is the stranger. Nothing is stranger or more alien than the other man, and it is in the light of utopia that one touches man outside of all rootedness and

---

5   "But art is disclosure of the being of the essent." Martin Heidegger: *Introduction to Metaphysics* (trans. Ralph Mannheim); Doubleday: New York.

domestication. Homelessness becomes the humanity of man—and not his degradation in the forgottenness of Being and the triumph of technique.

In this adventure where the I dedicates itself to the poem so as to meet the other in the non-place, it is the return that is surprising—a return based not on the response of the summoned relation, but on the circularity of the meridian—perfected trajectory of this movement without return—, which is the "finality without end" of the poetic movement. As if in going toward the other, I were reunited with myself and implanted myself in a soil that would, henceforth, be native; as if the distancing of the I drew me closer to myself, discharged of the full weight of my identity—a movement of which poetry would be the possibility itself, and a native land which owes nothing to rootedness, nothing to "prior occupation": a native land that has no need to be a birthplace. Native land or promised land? Does it spew forth its inhabitants when they forget the course of one who goes off in search of the other. Native land on the meridian—which is to say: a *here* which is also the *everywhere*, a wandering and expatriation to the point of depaganisation. Is the earth habitable otherwise? I do not see Celan's references to Judaism as some picturesque particular or familial lore. No doubt the Passion of Israel under Nazism (the theme of the twenty pages of "Strette" in *Strette*? lamentation of lamentations) has in the eyes—and the guts—of the poet a grave significance, but it is a significance which signifies for the human as such, of which Judaism is an extreme possibility—to the point of impossibility—a break with the naiveté of the shepherd, the herald, the messenger of Being.

A bursting open of Being which offers no rest, but only, to pass the night, stones against which strikes the stick of wandering, echoing in mineral language. Insomnia in the bed of Being, like the impossibility of curling up to shut one's eyes. Expulsion beyond the

59

"worldliness of the world"; nudity of him who borrows everything; insensibility to Nature "—for the Jew, you know, what does he really have that truly belongs to him, that isn't his on loan, borrowed and never given back...." We are once again in "Conversation in the Mountains."

Two Jews stand in the landscape evoked earlier by the turk's-cap and aphonic. "But they, the cousins germane, they have... no eyes" or, more exactly, for them a veil immediately covers any apparent image, "For the Jew and Nature, they are twofold, now too, even today, even here....Poor turk's-cap, poor aphonic!...you poor wretches, you do not stand and do not bloom, you are not present and July is not July." And those mountains in their majesty—what of those mountains of which Hegel said, with submission and liberty: "That's how it is"? Celan writes: "...the earth folded up here, folded once and twice and a third time, and opened up in the middle, and in the middle there is water, and the water is green, and the green is white, and the white comes from even further up, comes from the glaciers...."

There must be—beyond the silence and insignificance of a fold in the terrain, called "mountain," and beyond the sound of stick striking stone and stone echoing the sound—there must be, against "the language here" and beyond it—there must be a true word.

It cannot be doubted that, for Clean—in a world or a no world inconceivable for a Mallarmé—the poem is again the spiritual act *par excellence*: an act that is at once impossible and inevitable because of an "absolute poem" which "doesn't exist." Absolute: would this poem then speak the meaning of Being, "dwell poetically" with it, the *dichterisch wohnet der Mensch auf diesel Erde* of Holder in, wherein the Being of beings names itself? It speaks rather of the failure of all dimensionality and moves toward utopia. Infinitely less than the unfolding of Being, it undertakes "the impossible path, this path of the impossible...." "The absolute poem—no, it doesn't exist, it cannot exist." Is Celan speaking with gratuitous facility of some "unrealisable ideal"? Is he not suggesting a modality other than that of existence and nonexistence, other than all those that are to be found between these two limits? Does he not suggest poetry itself as an unheard modality, as an "otherwise than Being"?—The absolute poem does not exist: "But each real poem, even the least pretentious, contains this inescapable question, this incredible demand." A meridian—"like language, abstract, yet earthly...." An unavoidable questioning, interrupting the games of the beautiful, in search of the Other; a search dedicating itself in poem toward the Other: the song rises in the *giving*, in the one-for-the-other, in the very significance of signification—a significance which is older than ontology or the thinking of Being, and which is assumed by knowledge and desire, philosophy and libido.

translated from the French by Stephen Melville

VIGILOUS, REEL: DESIRE (A)S ACCUSATION

Nathanaël

Chaque fois, si fidèle qu'on veuille être, on est en train de trahir la singularité de l'autre à qui l'on s'adresse. Jacques Derrida

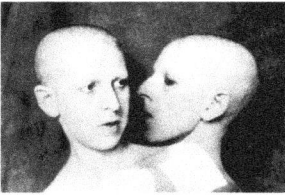

Que me veux-tu? (1928)

J'ouvre et je vois, j'appréhende, ce qui de moi n'est pas à moi et ne m'étant m'adresse une réplique catastrophée.[1]

To speak at the last; to take up speaking, this that is in my throat, and to give it to the space just beyond the mouth, to push past what resists speaking into address, a catch, lurch into the blasted architecture of language's predispositions, to speak, yes, say, to you, in address, each, without recrimination, I am bereft, not just, and unguarded, what *you* is spoken out of me into a cataleptic reel, disallowed and spleen, first, my disloyalties, and first again, in the shrapnelled everlast, my culpability. § None of it is unforeseen. What follows then is ever, always, incomplete.

---

1   I open and I see, I apprehend, that which of me is not mine and being not (of) me address myself a catastrophied retort.

Desire's accusations are irrefutable. I come to you with judgement and morbidity. Against a theatre of moveable parts, Genet insists "l'architecture du théâtre…doit être fixe, immobilisée, afin qu'on la reconnaisse responsable: elle sera jugée sur sa forme."[2] This, then, is my injunction, that I bring with me, my "irreversible"[3] theatre. § Judge me.

An "acte irreversible" may be a form of vigilance. An exacerbated attentiveness to vitality's decrepitude. § Surely, we are a wake, yes? The fantastical certitudes of presence are beguiling. But what of this: the torn-apart, seen, the over-seen and underwritten, they make perishable pledges. In the oxygenated body's (re)turn, there is already me against you against me: hard. Our vigilous turpitude.

It might be that in looking, the apprehensions are reinscribed. *Re*, because the intimations, indeed the intimidations, precede us. We anticipate them, we make them. That we are. We imagine them imaginable. Imago, each, insect-like and sexable, you and me. Genet again: "l'acte fixe qui se juge."[4]

---

2   Jean Genet, "L'étrange mot d'…", *Œuvres complètes IV*, Paris, Gallimard, 1968, p. 11 (*…the architecture of the theatre … must be fixed, immobilized, so that it can be recognized as responsible: it will be judged on its form.* Tr. Ch. Mandell, in *Fragments of the Artwork*, Stanford, 2003.). The full passage in question reads: "Où aller? Vers quelle forme? Le lieu théâtral, contenant l'espace scénique et la salle? // Le lieu. À un Italien qui voulait construire un théâtre dont les éléments seraient mobiles et l'architecture du théâtre est à découvrir, mais elle doit être fixe, immobilisée, afin qu'on la reconnaisse responsable: elle sera jugée sur sa forme. Il est trop facile de se confier au mouvant. Qu'on aille, si l'on veut, au périssable, mais après l'acte irréversible sur lequel nous serons jugé, ou, si l'on veut encore, l'acte fixe qui se juge. "

3   "Qu'on aille, si l'on veut, au périssable, mais après l'acte irréversible sur lequel nous serons jugé, ou, si l'on veut encore, l'acte fixe qui se juge." *Ibid.*

4   …the fixed act that judges itself. *Ibid.*

§ *Fixe*.

A form for looking, *je te fixe*, I stare at you. And if looking, *fixer*, to stare, *fixate*, is judgement, then this meeting is irrepressibly (ir)responsible. It is possible that these attentions that summon, the manifestations of presence, in part, are transliterations of belated, sometimes blatant, violence. From mouth to morsel. Might we, in keeping with our selves, do our best to fall apart? Our best kept. And sacriledge. § Lie to me. Tell me what you want.

That form and act enact de-formity. It is this, I think, that is a/e motion. With Buber, I concur, emphatically: "it does not help you to survive."[5] Is that what we are here for? Over-life? (*Sur-vie?*) This is its disparity—and disparage. (Recalling now that *parages* in French are the outskirts, the outwards of a place, beyond a circumscribed area, unmapped, but sensed, intimated, and it is this, intimate, these intimacies, these topographical skirtings which arouse my sensibilities, interpellate me overly: I go. *Dis*-paraging.)

§ Accusative.[6]

---

5   *I and Thou*, tr. W. Kaufmann, New York: Scribner's, 1970, 84.

6   *Accusative, a.* 1. *Grammar.* In inflected languages the name of the case whose primary function was to express destination or the goal of motion; hence the case which follows prepositions implying motion towards, and expresses the object of transitive verbs, i.e. the destination of the verbal action; sometimes applied, in uninflected languages, to the *relation* in which the object stands, as shown by its position alone. By omission of the word *case, accusative* is commonly used substantively. 2. (From <u>ACCUSE</u> *v.*) Pertaining, tending, or addicted to accusation; accusatory. *Obs. rare.* (*Oxford English Dictionary Online*, 2009.)

Lacan contends: "Le désir s'ébauche dans la marge où la demande se déchire du besoin."[7] Desire's recriminations reel. They are junctive and enfold. If the body's edge is unintelligibly marginal, then desire might be its marginalia—*sexed text*. Whatever its outpouring, origination. In an invented etymology of dis-parage, the act, if this were an act with form—*begging judgement, responsibility*—the act, then, would entail the undoing (*dis*) of its sensed and sensory outwards (*parage*): its skin, if you will, peeled back: flayed. § Is this what it is to be denuded—*proteus*, of inconstant form – quickened?

These are desire's hermaphrodisms, counter-sexed, unchecked, in pieces on the floor. Demand rent from need makes a seam up the middle of me. It is here that I mis-dream the dream of what Buber calls "the double cry." Echo ingested and thrown down, undaunted. Woken, what sleeps, seeps from dream, de-means: *Que me veux-tu? What do you want from me?*

There it is, demonstrably: demand ripped away from need. In Claude Cahun's double exposure, the twain self is put to the test of its (ir)reversibility, face to face, conjunctive, obliterative fixation: split at the point of seeing. What vigil does (s)he keep? Onanistic wounding, it is the body severed from itself, rejoined, twixt, tribadic, (s)he is all skin, undercut, misgiven. Dualling herself. Here, in the locked-down body-part, is the (im)parting of history that goes ungiven, dis(ap)proving its acts.

---

7   Jacques Lacan, « Subversion du sujet et dialectique du désir dans l'inconscient freudien », in *Écrits II*, Paris: Seuil, 1971. 174. (*Desire begins to take shape in the margin in which demand rips away from need*. tr. B. Fink, *Écrits: A Selection*, New York/London: Norton, 2002. 814)

§ Act.

Objection: Is equal parts objected and abjected, simultaneous parsings of misspeaking. *Que me veux-tu?* is already vanquished, exposure, its architecture unconditionally disastered. *What do you want from me* might be *want me* overturned, *veux* en a verge of *veulerie*, accusing despondent refusal, here, with me. A surge of deadliness, a self with its sorrow rubbing the malignant parts, propagating a heedless rush of disintegrations which start small and become smaller and smaller and more deadly, particulate. What sees seeing is a morbid intimation, a cast-off accent, an accident of being, where what passes passes on. And we are (with) it. With: conjoined, vestigial. In Cahun's splittings, reflective echoings of self with self, this ontological distressor undresses the eyes that look not-looking. Our eyes, and it comes at me like this, with the full throttle of history slammed against an unprepared ground. If only it would shatter. If only it would bleed.

     *

The conditional is bereaved: tense, unappeased. It carries potentiality's breach, boring into the undetermined with disbelief. The *if then* of me, constructed such that uncertainty, embedded in the causal palate of language's misdeed, is militantly rejected by a structuring of sated need. It locks into place, but this does nothing for a body that falls from a sky. The contaminant is alive, it is vital, distressed; it disregards our posturings. "Rien n'est vrai," contends Édouard Glissant, "tout est vivant." It is this untrue-alive, which is the end of I (*je*)—its everlast. The insistence of Cahun's intransigeant interrogation, speaking, alive: what want and to what end this accusation of endings? Each thing in ending, at the very start. It is sometimes called: onset. And we are its disease.

Cioran calls it fear: "La peur de la mort n'est que la projection dans l'avenir d'une peur qui remonte à notre premier instant."[8] *Fear of death is merely the projection into the future of a fear which dates back to our first moment of life.*[9] "Le mal," he insists, "le vrai mal est pourtant *derrière*, non devant nous."[10] Le mal is also malady, affliction. It touches the last in anticipation, it staggers at our outwards, screwing the self to its ghastly (dis)appearance. This is not timorosity—unless it is a permeated vocable, with its suggestions of rashness (*temerousness*), gravity (*morosity*) and insistence (*temerity*); it is what it calls up without speaking a word. Cahun's photographic vigil is death's abandon, the halting of temporal extravagance; it is neither beginning's end, nor end's beginning, but the monumental ripping apart of history's seams, seemingly: a catastrophic forethought unwound in the body's appellate appeal. Death's unwieldy divide.

Unchaste it bemoans its (mis)demeanor. The clasped features pursed at the threshold of an imperiled, contrary kiss: might this be its admission? § If we come running, it is to see past the lurch of the thing coming at us, past mirror, ill-reflected, concomitant sequence of disappearance, in which the photograph *reproduces* what it rebukes, forcing *it* out of *it*self, unquelled fornicant. What

---

8   *De l'inconvénient d'être né*, Paris: Gallimard, 1973. 10. "Fear of death is merely the projection into the future of a fear which dates back to our first moment of life."

9   Tr. Richard Howard, *The Trouble with Being Born*, 4.

10   *Ibid.* "Yet evil, the real evil, is *behind*, not ahead of us."

doesn't last, mimicry of a kindred, menacing other-kind. Replica, a falsehood, which begs the French *réplique*, the aftershock of a kind of speaking, on a stage, in a residual theatre: the re-hearsals of repetition (practice), in which the manifold face is disregarded and its traits. Viscera.

At the point of suture, breasts striking one another, clavicles fastened, thighs sewn to groin, bones grafted together, something incoheres. I want to say *self*, the (un)(m)asked *je*, in ambiguity, but it is in the mouth, I hear it, the mouth, in speaking, jeers. *Que me veux-tu?* rips it apart. The melded together form is an amorous atrocity. Think past the raced two-backed beast ahead to Mengele's stitchings, botched clonings, the quiet explosions in each carcinogened throat. This too is closed. Closed against a century come screeching to a shrapnelled halt. It is from this that we are thrown up, detritus, up-heaval, and this is as I look back. Celan made it that far, tracking language's fission, the determined destruction of speech, perenially unwitnessed, obliviated, still. Demanding: "Speak, you also, / speak as the last, / have your say. // Speak— / But keep yes and no unsplit."[11] Unsplit—negation and acquiescence, act and form, judgement and responsibility, speaking and seeing: twice swallowed back, twice more.

Unsplit—fissive—is Cahun's duplicitous duplication. *Que me veux-tu?* is the resilient outwardness of the *moi-je*, its act of aggressive fortress, the imparting of its grievance: this too is (un)given. An introverted address, delivered against a self of severalness. Here (in the body), the accusative other is a surrogate admonishment. The speaking to-against self is menially obliterative—self-speaking

---

11   "Sprich Auch Du / Speak, You Also", in *Poems of Paul Celan*, tr. Michael Hamburger. New York: Persea, 1995 (1972). 100-101.

for self-seeing in history's optic disallows an iteration other than grief's opportunism: the self-same is the having been. It calls out its lastness, makes itself echo and chamber, absorbing shadow into shadowy light: "Where death is! Alive!"[12]

If it is true that "Le désir est mort, tué par une image,"[13] it may be that this accusatively emphatic image bespeaks the murderous vigil; to watch, unbidden. To bring the body, unworn, to testify against itself, to responsibilise its enmity, build up the wall of its own figuration, severely, make what is seen visible against history's rent screen—a black box of miserly misery. Speak into speaking, unlistened. § I go to where it happens. The door is a door that closes. A gate that scrapes shut against a forensic, vaulted compound. These are its barbed technologies, its unmitigated heat, a fire that doesn't burn, a blood that doesn't bleed: the smell of it. If desire is dead it is dead at the point of seeing, accused, beseeching. It dies undead, it sees unspoken, it works its asphyxiation into the endangered throat, stripped of its vital civility, mouth open on no sound, untold. The wither image may have killed desire, ineradicably. Death's death as it were, remaindered at its skinned edge, its posthumous (re)iteration, end upon devastated end.

The photograph is fixed. It is what we see Claude Cahun foreseeing, our looking back, Orphic, and (s)he is beside herself. Fixed is also contrived. It is volatility's compression, the arrestation of dislocation. The fleeting self, refined. Along with the rest of us, purged of our purities. Our changeability is incumbent upon it. There upon Genet's

---

12   Celan, *ibid.*

13   Marguerite Duras, *Le Navire Night*, Paris: Mercure de France, 1986 (1979). 52 (*Desire is dead; the image killed it.*).

69

shattered columbarium is ethics's structural impediment. The sanguine, greedy respite from being. The graves he has us digging (up). § I go there. I take you with me. I wear it out. I wipe it back. I die your death. With the mechanisms of futility. The egregious armatures. A body carried out. *It* overtakes me.

*

This is address's vigil. Stood up against speaking, the body closes its eyes against a fixed theatre with its morbid charge of desirability. Our reciprocal fixation is foregone. With martial ease, when we meet. We are inseparable in our imminence, and our defeat. *Que me veux-tu?* realigns these empathic defections, forcing agonic substance out, and the languages we mis-speak. The blood of it is thick in me. With you, I am suspect, here in this theatre.

N
Chicago, November 2009

Author's note: This talk was first delivered December 2, 2009 at Universität Wien in the context of the "Queer Interventions" lecture series. To Elisabeth Tutschek, Astrid Fellner and Eugen Banauch, for their kind hospitality. To Stephen Motika, Benny Nemerofsky Ramsay, Christine Stewart, and Brian Teare for their vigilation.

LORINE NIEDECKER
HARMONIZING WITH PAUL CELAN

Elizabeth Robinson

We both know that the fugue is waterborne. The neologism

of the buoyant, or its compound word, the slant

rhyme of those who sink.

    Scrub the floors.

    Chew the sleepcorn.

All our mothers are dead or deaf. All our masters

sing the flood. The rise

in the word, the hermetic correspondence

we drowned before exchange. The penultimate

breath, your golden air.

PAUL CELAN AND LANGUAGE

Jacques Derrida

Q: Would you say that one must have been, like Celan maybe, capable of living the death of language in order to try to render that experience "live"?

A: It seems to me that he had to live that death at each moment. In several ways. He must have lived it everywhere where he felt that the German language had been killed in a certain way, for example by subjects of the German language who made a specific use of it: the language is manhandled, killed, put to death because it is made to say in this or that way. The experience of Nazism is a crime against the German language. What was said in German under Nazism is a death. There is another death, namely the banalization, the trivialization of language, of the German language for example, anywhere, anytime. And then there is another death, which is the one that cannot not happen to language because of what it is, that is to say: repetition, slide into lethargy, mechanization, etcetera. The poetic act thus constitutes a kind of resurrection: the poet is someone who is permanently involved with a language that is dying and which he resurrects, not by giving it back some triumphant aspect but by making it return sometimes, like a specter or a ghost: the poet wakes up language and in order to really make the "live" experience of this making up, of this return to life of language, one has to be very close to the corpse of the language. One has to be as close as possible to its remains. I wouldn't want to give in to pathos too much here, but I suppose that Celan had constantly to deal with a language that was in danger of becoming a dead language. The poet is someone who notices that language, that his language, the language he inherits in the sense I mentioned earlier, risks becoming a dead language again and that therefore he has the responsibility, a very grave responsibility, to wake it up, to resuscitate it (not in the sense of Christian glory but in the sense of the resurrection of language), neither as an immortal body nor as a glorious body but as a mortal body, fragile and at times indecipherable, as is each poem by Celan. Each poem is a resurrection, but one that engages us with a vulnerable body that may yet again slip into oblivion. I believe that in a certain way all of Celan's poems remain indecipherable, keep some indecipherability, and this indecipherability can either call interminably for a sort of reinterpretation, a resurrection, new breaths of interpretation or fade away, perish again. Nothing insures a poem against its death, because its archive can always be burned in crematory ovens or in house fires, or because, without being burned, it is simply forgotten, or not interpreted or permitted to slip into lethargy. Forgetting is always a possibility.

translated from the French by Pierre Joris

THE MEMORY OF WORDS

Edmond Jabès

I have never spoken of Paul Celan. Modesty? Inability to read his language? And yet everything draws me to him.

I love the man who was my friend. And, in their differences, our books meet up.
The same questioning links us, the same wounded word.

I have never written anything on Paul Celan. Today I take the risk of doing so. I did not make this decision all alone.
To write for the first time on Paul Celan, for German readers, tempted me.[1]
To write for the first time on Paul Celan and to give my writing as destination the place opened by his language, by his very words, has convinced me to say "yes"—as one says "yes" to oneself, in silence or in solitude. While thinking, however, about the missing friend. And as if, for the first time, serenely, I accompanied him there where we had never penetrated together, into the very heart of the language with which he had battled so fiercely and which was not the one in which we spoke to each other.

To whom to speak when the other no longer is?
The place is empty when emptiness occupies all of the place.
Paul Celan's voice reading in my house, for me, some of his poems, has never fallen silent. I hear it, at this very moment when, pen in hand, I listen to my words going toward his. I listen to his words in mine, as one listens to the heartbeat of a person one has not

---

1   Asked to do so by the *Frankfurter Allgemeine Zeitung.*

left, in the shadow where, henceforth, he stands.

This voice is at the center of the reading I do of his poems; for I can read Paul Celan only in translation; but through the means I have given myself to approach his texts, helped by the poet's unforgettable voice, most of the time I have the sense of not betraying him.

Paul Celan himself was an admirable translator.

One day, when I told him I had trouble recognizing the poems he was reading to me in the French translations I was looking at—there were few of them in 1968—he said that on the whole he was satisfied with those translations.

"Translation"—as the poet Philippe Soupault wrote in his preface to Prince Igor—"is treason only when it pretends, like photography, to reproduce reality. It would mean to decide beforehand that a text has neither relief, nor harmonics, nor colors, nor, before all, rhythm."

It's true; but what then happens to the original text?

The satisfaction Paul Celan expressed concerning the translations, published or about to be published, puzzled me. "It is difficult to do any better," he would add. Is it because, deep inside himself, he knew, better than any other writer, that he was an untranslatable author?

Behind the language of Paul Celan lies the never extinguished echo of another language.

Like us, skirting before crossing at a certain hour of the day the border of shadow and light, the words of Paul Celan move and affirm themselves at the edge of two languages of the same size— that of renouncement and that of hope.

A language of poverty, a language of riches.

On one side, clarity; on the other, obscurity. But how to distinguish between them when they are blended to such a degree?

Glorious morning or mournful evening? Neither the one nor the other, but—inexpressible pain—the vast and desolate field wrapped in fog, of what cannot express itself alone, outside and in time.

Neither day nor night, then, but by means of their conjugated voices, the undefined space, left vacant by the retreat of the dispossessed language at the core of the refound language.

And as if that word could raise itself only on the ruins of the other, with and without it.

Dust, dust.

Silence, as all writers know, allows the word to be heard. At a given moment, the silence is so strong that the words express nothing but it alone.

Does this silence, capable of making language tilt over, possess its own language to which one can attribute neither origin nor name?

Inaudible language of the secret?

Those who have been reduced to silence, once, know it best, but know also that they can hear it, can understand it only through the words of the language they work in.

Uninterrupted passage from silence to silence and from word to silence.

But the question remains: is the language of silence that of the refusal of language or, to the contrary, the language of the memory of the first word?

Didn't we know it? The word which is formed by letters and sounds keeps the memory of the school book or of any other book that revealed it to us one day, revealed it, by revealing it to itself; keep the memory, also, of all the voices that over the course of years—and even centuries—have pronounced and spread it.

Words discovered or transmitted by foreign or familiar

hands, by distant or close voices, voices from yesterday, sweet to the ear or cruel and feared.

There is, I am certain, no history of the word; but there is a history of the silence every word narrates.

The words saying only that silence. Theirs and ours.

To interrogate a writer means first of all to interrogate the words of his memory, the words of his silence; to tunnel down into their past as "vocables"—the words are older than us and the text has no age.

For Paul Celan the German language, though it is the one in which he immersed himself, is also the one which for a time those who claimed to be its protectors had forbidden him.

If it is indeed the language of his pride, it is also that of his humiliation. Isn't it with the words of his allegiance that they had tried to tear him from himself and to abandon him to solitude or errancy, not having managed to hand him over to death immediately?

There is something paradoxical to stand suddenly alien to the world and to totally invest yourself in the language of a country that rejects you, to the point of claiming that language for yourself alone.

As if the language belonged truly only to those who love it beyond anything else and feel riveted to it forever.

Strange passion, which has for itself only the strength and determination of its own passion.

Stéphane Moses notes in his analysis of "Conversations in the Mountains" that in this poem Celan's use of certain expressions borrowed from Judeo-German could well be on his part a challenge to the executioner.

This does not seem evident to me.

The challenge to the executioner lies elsewhere. It resides in the very language of the poetry. A language he has lifted to its summits.

The constant battle that every writer fights with the words to force them to express his deepest intimacy, no one lived it as desperately in his own body, lived, it doubly, as did Paul Celan.

To know how to glorify the word that kills us. To kill the word that saves us and glorifies us.

The love-hate relationship with the German language led him toward the end of his life to write poems of which one can only read the tearing.

Hence the reader's difficulty to approach them straight on.

In his first poems Paul Celan is carried by the words of the language of his thought and of his breath: the language of his soul.

He is in need of this language in order to live. His life is written, in the language of his writing, with the words of his life itself and with those of death, which is a further word.

In his last poems the relentlessness he musters against it reaches its peak. To die at the heart of his love.

To destroy what tries to say itself, before saying it; as if now silence alone had the right to be there: this silence from before and after the words, this silence between the words, between two languages, arrayed one against the other and yet promised to the same fate.

All his poetry was a search for a reality. The reality of a language? The real is the absolute.

To confront his executioners in the name of the language they share with him, and to force them to their knees.

That was the major bet, held.

If to translate is, truly, to betray, do I dare admit that, in order to hear Paul Celan better, I have taken the road of treason?

But isn't every personal reading in itself an act of treason?

Incapable of reading directly in German, I read Paul Celan in his various translations: French, English, or Italian. All acceptable. All insufficient but permitting a better comprehension of the original text. What one lacks, the other helps me to grasp better.

I read these translations without ever losing sight of the German text, trying to discover in it the rhythm, the movement, the music, the caesura. Guided by the accurate voice of Paul Celan. Hadn't he himself initiated me into this reading?

All the languages that I know help me enter into his, which I don't know. By this rare, unusual detour I come as close as possible to his poetry.

Have I ever read Paul Celan? I have listened to him for a long time. I listen to him. Each time his books renew a dialogue the beginning of which I can't remember, though nothing has come to interrupt it since then.

Silent dialogue through words as light as free and adventurous birds; all the world's gravity being in the sky; like stones laid by nostalgic ghosts on the marble of nonexistent tombs; all the world's pain being in the earth; and like ashes of an interminable day of horror of which there remains but the unbearable image of pink smoke above millions of burned bodies.

A nothing rose
a Noone's Rose

A nothing
were we, are we, will

we remain, blossoming:
the nothing—, the
noonesrose.

translated from the French by Pierre Joris

SPEECH

Hadara Bar-Nadav

I have come to you
                  alone

     a green
          word

     growing
     an inward landscape

The force   I believe
     I have been conversing in

is human

An erasure of Paul Celan's "The Meridian" fom *Selected Poems and Prose of Paul Celan*, trans. John Felstiner (Norton, 2001).

MEDITATIONS ON THEM AND
THE EARTH INSIDE THEM THAT THEY DUG

Dan Beachy-Quick

§

Some poems contain ontologies. Some poems contain theogonies. Some poems swallow Adam and Eve and remove them from their names. Some poems swallow the world to ask a question about what the world may be.

Some poems swallow God.

Some poems, in order to become poems, must begin at the beginning. When there is no place to begin such a poem must forge a place of beginning. Such poems begin in fact. Here is a fact: "There was earth inside them, and"—and here is a response to fact the fact alone makes possible: "they dug."

§

We think—this we that holds the book in which we read the poem—the earth is what is outside of us. This poem tells us we are wrong. The earth is in them and so too the earth is in us.

To find the earth we dig in ourselves. To dig in ourselves is to find the earth by removing it. Creation begins by creating within oneself nothing.

Creation is a form of work that doesn't feel like creation. It feels like work.

§

Who is God? God is who knows. God is who wants.

Does God do the work? God knows the work is being done.

God is one who is none.

§

They do not grow wise. What is wisdom? Wisdom is when one drops the tool in one's hand. Wisdom is a question one asks about the work when one has decided the work is done. This is work that is not done.

They invent no song. What is song? Song celebrates work being over. This is work that is not done.

They think for themselves no language. What is language for? For describing the work when the work is over. Language presupposes the past tense. In words the present tense is already over even as the event occurs. Here there is no language they speak. They dig.

§

The storms fill stillness with oceans. An ocean is water in a hole.

Creation requires nothing, and then it requires separation. They become you and I. There is no world if one cannot become two. What's at stake? The world's at stake. The worm digs with them, turning dead matter over into fecundity. Digging in the dirt they make the dirt in which they dig. *Earth came of earth.*

I don't want to reduce my own digging to paraphrase. But I want to point out, to myself as to you, that they did not sing the song that sings them. No. "That singing out there says: They dig."

It is the singing that says.

§

Many songs begin: O, _____. [Fill in the blank.]

Every song begins by filling in the blank.

O is an expression that encircles blankness to let itself be heard.

§

To be forced to ask basic questions, questions that work against the answers they seem to suggest. How does language come of use in the poem?

Here is a poem of simple words: pronouns and nouns and verbs. Here is them, here is earth, here is them digging, here is us with them in the earth. Here is this them that is also an I and a you. Here is an I am that the poem turns into an us. Now I am us. Here is God who is no one. Here is the mouth in praise or in pain saying O—a shape the mouth makes that mimics the letter that signifies the sound of its own utterance. O. O you. O you, who put on the ring once, put on the ring again. The ring, too, is an O.

The poem, too, is an O. It circles itself to form a world, and then the language that draws the boundary enters into the field it limned and comes of use. O is its own paradox. They can only speak in this world the words that make this world possible. They are themselves these words they must also speak. But they do not speak, they dig. It is "that singing out there says: They dig." O reference. O sense. O it is not praise; it is work. O, dig.

§

That which is blank must precede the mark that ends its blankness. Blankness is a form of zero, of nothing, of absence. The page and the earth are both forms of blankness.

The figure O places a mark on blankness by embracing nothing. Outside the boundary of the line is the old absence; within the boundary of the line, brought full circle, is an absence found within absence, a deeper nothing discovered by marking nothing as a surface on which we dig. O is the open mouth of the tunnel. O is the eye within whose white circle is a circle made of absence in which light digs. O is the shape of the hole.

§

The desire to say something true undermined by desire or truth.

Where is the earth? Inside us.

§

How desperately I want to think in order to avoid conclusion. Is this the same as asking a question? I don't know. At the end of our work "the ring awakes." The ring is an O. O is the beginning of prayer and the beginning of lament. O is also a sign of betrothal.

Betrothal to what? To us? Who are we? If the finger is "ours" to whom does it belong? The finger that wears the ring is not yours or mine. The eye is a ring when it opens. The end of our work is the ring that awakes. What does it wake to? What does it wake us to? A world, maybe. Not conclusion. To be in the world is for us to be devoted to it. This work is our devotion. Our work, and only our work, our digging down into the mouth of nothing awakes us to all. What is the figure of that all? A ring, an O. (Think of the planet drawn by a child, a line in two dimensions; think of the sun in full eclipse.) It all makes an absence we put our finger through.

World, mouth, eye, ring—underneath their meaning they are the same word. O they are what they sing. They sing us. To put our finger through is to wake up.

THERE WAS EARTH INSIDE THEM

Paul Celan

There was earth inside them, and
they dug.

They dug and dug, and so
their day went past, their night. And they did not praise God,
who, so they heard, wanted all this,
who, so they heard, witnessed all this.

They dug and heard nothing more;
they did not grow wise, invented no song,
devised for themselves no sort of language.
They dug.

There came a stillness then, came also storm,
all of the oceans came.
I dig, you dig, and it, the worm, digs too,
and the singing there says: They dig.

O one, O none, O no one, O you:
Where did it go, then, making for nowhere?
O you dig and I dig, and I dig through to you,
and the ring on our finger awakens.

translated from the German by John Felstiner

BROT UND ROSEN

Aleš Šteger

Although the January wind did not whirl it out of the past, but, still
fresh from this moment's creation, out of our cerebral landscape,
memory's pale cloud filled the whole afternoon. Or was it just the
smell of cigars floating between the word *bread* and the word *roses*
in the restaurant? And was this floating later filed away with the
inscription *remembered* or with the inscription *invented*? Why waste
so many words over the dryness of tobacco, unless words are found
in the middle of what's lost? Only once have they managed to hide,
but my interlocutor Triton stirred them to the surface again, stabbing
under thin slices of carpaccio with a fork. He put down the cutlery,
looked through the window leaning against my back with its poor
evening light, challenging me like a duelist. He was talking about the
Friedrichshain district where we were sitting, about the final street
combat, which raged here in April of '45. Russian units were biting
into the city like circular saws. The less dazzled commanders of the
SS detachments ordered the rest of the soldiers, most of them under
sixteen, to retreat. Retreat, as far west as possible. Better to fall into
the hands of the Americans than the Russians. Only small children
were safe from Russian vengeance, he said, because the Russians
were exceptionally violent and melodramatic at the same time. And
there was more than enough of both, violence and melodrama, in
the twentieth century. The twentieth century. As I turned to measure
the evening behind the window, hundreds of summers and winters
were falling from the sky, white and slow like porcelain. In Dresden
it shattered like the body in the body of his grandmother, who was
gang raped during the invasion. Is he allowed, as a German, as the
executioners' son, to write of the aggression of the victims? Is poetry
an accounting, is it testimony? And if so, is it only the testimony
of the victors? Is it a rhythmically captive memory? Is it a rhymed

draining of ethics and ideology? Or is it a parallel world, a vent for the acrobatics of the liberated imagination? Is a poem allowed to testify about something passed along as some story? What we have experienced only as someone else's memory? Not in the images on the retina and the vibrations of the eyes, only in the echo of babble, in the desperate whisper, the coming and going of borrowed words? And is a poem, because of the *if it* tattooed on the arm, is a poem not only for amusement? If you could become someone else for an hour, whom would you choose? Donald Rumsfeld. And Hitler? For an hour, for an hour you would. Did you know: the name of the man who cremated Adolf was Faust? And he was Jewish, of course. What did Auden say about Rilke? That he was the greatest lesbian poet after Sappho. And what did Brecht say about Rilke? That whenever he talks about god, he gets a faggy look on his face. And outside it was snowing. And outside it was snowing. Poetry is like a cocoon, said my interlocutor, and lit another cigar. Now it has shut again. It's been like this for three thousand years. The shifting movement between phases, when it is a princess and when it is an orphan. Now we are in the waiting phase again. A hundred years ago in Switzerland, Nietzsche, too, gave a lecture to four students, two of whom were homeless, escaping to the lecture room because of the harsh winter. This is why it does not hurt that a collection of verses does not raise interest like a novel does. That poetry is currently not in the condition to undermine the system. That it does not yield as much financially, that smarts, he added. Or did I add it myself? My memory is slowly deserting me. I remember I ordered whiskey and wine once again and said that poetry furthermore was sometimes a cocoon and sometimes a butterfly, also at times Maya the bee, at times the computer game of a daydreamer, at times a mass grave. I don't know where Odysseus, Saint Paul, and Schopenhauer, the last a little less holy, edged into our conversation from. At midnight

89

we were separated by religion, ahead of which I had emigrated
and to which he had made a pilgrimage. Meanwhile outside it was
snowing. As we said goodbye, it already had covered all the folds
and falls. The traces of shrapnel and grenades were not recognizable.
Everywhere only the white softness into which night was soundlessly
falling. I stopped by a certain tavern and ordered another for across.
Then I trudged through the snow with heavy tread towards the empty
Alexanderplatz. When I looked back, there was not even a thread of
my path behind me.

translated from the Slovenian by Brian Henry

Notes: *Brot und Rosen* is the name of a restaurant in Berlin. The German
poet Durs Grünbein has written a book called *Porcelain*, which also
conjures "pour Celan." Grünbein also has published the book *Falten und
Fallen*, or *Folds and Falls*. From *Berlin* (Beletrina, 2007), pages 48-50.

PSALM

Joshua Corey

Neiman Marcus knits a leader out of earth and lime.
Neiman be-shops a western stab.
Neiman.

Galloped apts do, Neiman.
Dear zoo leads woolens
to veer bloomers.
Dear
engager.

Nine naughts:
where we're singed, we're wared,
we're weary bluehound.
Deathnaut dreading
kneed man's rose.

Mid-
den grin seals in hell
dem stabled-faded him's liverwurst,
dares crone's rot.
Vow the pupa's word. Dazzled weresong.
Or bear, O you bar
the door.

PSALM

Paul Celan

translated by John Felstiner

No one kneads us again out of earth
and clay,
no one incants our dust.
No one.

Blessèd art thou, No One.
In thy sight would
we bloom.
In thy
spite.

A Nothing
we were, are now, and ever
shall be, blooming:

Niemand knetet uns wieder aus Erde
und Lehm,
niemand bespricht unsern Staub.
Niemand.

Gelobt seist du, Niemand.
Dir zulieb wollen
wir blühn.
Dir
entgegen.

Ein Nichts
waren wir, sind wir, warden
wir bleiben, blühend:

die Nichts-, die
Niemandsrose.

Mit
dem Griffel seelenhell,
dem Staubfaden himmelswüst,
der Krone rot
vom Purpurwort, das wir sangen
über, o über
dem Dorn.

the Nothing-, the
No-One's-Rose.

With
our pistil soul-bright,
our stamen heaven-waste,
our corona red
from the purpleword, we sang
over, O over
the thorn.

CONSTELLATIONS FOR THEREMIN

Andrew Joron

Poppy and Remembrance
– Celan

Dream-herb
– Goll

This cycle of twelve prose poems offers a commentary on, and a translation of, certain passages from the poems of Paul Celan and Yvan Goll—namely, those passages submitted as evidence of Celan's alleged plagiarism of Goll.

The charges against Celan are examined most thoroughly—and refuted unconditionally—in an article by Reinhard Döhl in the 1960 *Jahrbuch* of the Deutsche Akademie für Sprache und Dichtung. The epigraphs below, presenting twelve "parallel instances" wherein Celan's lines seem to echo Goll's, have been drawn from this article.

Rather than confirming plagiarism, the "parallel instances" testify to a marvellous confluence between Celan's early and Goll's late work. In the wake of the controversy, however, this moment of solidarity— of mutual inspiration—between the two poets has been minimized. Yet it is worth remembering that Celan personally delivered a copy of his first book to Goll and so initiated an earnest exchange of texts and talks. Celan recalls in a letter (to Alfred Margul-Sperber) that he visited Goll "many times," even as Goll's leukemia worsened. On these occasions, Celan would read his new work aloud to the dying poet. According to Celan, "The fact that Goll, who for many years hadn't written in German, began, before his death, to write in

German again, is due in no small measure to his connection with me and my poems."

Consequently, the echoic qualities of the passages in question must be understood in a redemptive light, as examples of Breton's alchemical *vases communicants*. To recover and reintegrate the utopian substance of these wounded words, an elaborate apparatus has been assembled here.

Its main component is the theremin, the electronic lyre of the Russian Revolution. This instrument is equipped with two antennas that generate an electromagnetic field; the performer's hands, without touching any surface, move within the field in an artful manner, causing a ripple of interference that, in turn, stimulates an oscillator to produce musical tones. The vital power radiated by the antique *kithara*—to animate stones (Amphion's lyre) or to rescue the dead (Orpheus's lyre)—is ascribed here to the theremin.

The epigraphs are intended, therefore, to function as the antennas of an imaginary theremin. Their "etheric waves" cascade over the body of the text below, activating its constituent elements. (The text is made up of both commentaries and translations. The latter derive from the same poems as the epigraphs and are marked by quotes. Translations from Goll's source-poems are given in the third paragraph of each section; from Celan's, in the fourth. But these boundaries are not impermeable, and phrases from the source-poems are liable to circulate throughout each section.)

Caught in an etheric field, the translations and commentaries interact as "constellations," in Benjamin's sense of a non-hierarchical, indeed, a *salvational* structure of thought. At once philosophical and poetical, the constellation unites—without abolishing the differences between—its nodal elements. It is a necessarily musical relation that prefigures the moment of reconciliation.

with birds in his hair he goes forth
– Celan

Your flesh of rose – your hair of birds
– Goll

That birds become points or musical notes; & that hair, horizontal lines or staves...

Hands are entangled in a force field to make music.
Hands are birds caught in the hair of the theremin.

"The closer I approach you, the more you sink into the abyss of preexistant objects."

"In vain you paint hearts on the window: a god goes among the hordes."

Flights of birds tune the strings of a destroyed or not-yet-invented instrument.

Pictures of ancient noise, hieratic news. Suggesting hair, birds, & the blue banners of the invisible.

the mills of death
– Celan

The Mill of Death
– Goll

A wheel-inhabited house. That adversary knows only advance: that cycle moves as this sickle.

Alter, altar. All beyond feeling, number than Blakean number, blacker than fact or factory.

"The fire turns pale, along with the water. There, on death's negative, blanches the cedar with carbonized branches."

"...doing the work better left to one's star."

That which spreads "beneath mammalian sleep"; that which swears "loudly from the rooftops of dreamless sleep."

As a theremin quotes from the Book of Disquiet: to see the sun at night, the eye pours out its contents.

A necklace of hands
– Celan

A necklace of larksongs
– Goll

The first book holds the letters of the last. Never to be corrected or corrupted, but thrown into the mouth of earth.

Memory is reduced to monument; unseen weight that bends the poppy, a perennial herb with milky juice, also known as the dreaming herb.

"We walk toward the single great eye that hangs over clouds in the forehead of a sullen thinker."

"Shells do I utter and thin clouds, and a hull sprouts in the rain. . . Black the portal springs open, I sing."

Fate foretold in tallow light: "silent circling lamps" lend a deeper hue to the jar of wasps, the bottle of air.

Voice, never-arrivingwave. The sound of the theremin sorrows over the absolute whiteness of the sick man's blood.

blood-ray of the moon
– Celan

a drop of moon-blood
– Goll

Cast into temporal waters, the bright broken images seek to rejoin, to become Original.

What lies open to reflection? The unanswered word, the world before it was made.

"Your foot will forget its way of going...planted my herb potent with magic....You must love me whether you want to or not."

"We say obscure things to one another, we love one another like poppy and remembrance."

"It's time that it was time" to drink one red drop, to sleep as wine in the shells.

See the sea misalign its mimic heaven! Song for theremin: "We are friends." Voice, never-returning wave.

In the form of a wild boar
your dream stamps through the woods at evening's edge.
– Celan

The wild boars with magical triangular heads
They stamp through my decaying dreams
– Goll

Magic cannot be seen or named. Better to banish the word, or show how black sublates white: as the German *rein*, the French *rien*.

Consider the line, with its mutually exclusive endpoints. To be exiled is the true homecoming. What, then, is the nature of self-evidence?

"And you and I with starry crowns: Proof eternal against the doom of time."

"So that a ripening like yours will enrapture the festive Eye that has wept such stones."

In this tale of the body, errors accumulate without fail. Victory tomorrow will be measured by the sun's refusal to rise.

Slavery will end, as the peripatetic argued, when the Loom weaves without a hand to guide it, or when the Lyre plays itself.

101

the mauve-colored death
– Celan

la mort violette
– Goll

To observe the paradox of a death *qui porte un nom de fleur*, divide appearance from its petal.

Then gaslights will burn as "reverberant flowers whose bereavement is mauve" or "wakeful flowers of the first sleep of the dead."

You, the other, always died. As someone said, "with a French heart, a German mind, and Jewish blood." But "you did not die the mauve-colored death."

You awaited the half-night's "dream-daggers," giving a "cry not from pain." After fighting your way deeper down, liberated, you were found by a fisherman on the holiday of revolution.

If there is a word that marks the place where language was born, it is "you."

Violated / violet. Now everything has been said: the theremin modulates as ethereal violin, fantastic prayer.

seven hearts later the hand knocks at the gate,
seven roses later the fountain splashes.
– Celan

You have seven hearts, queen,
They are all ignited
And compose my crown
– Goll

As talk, forced bleeding through higher dimensions, evolves toward typography, limbs pinned awkwardly to thin air.

Out of sequence, a Nilotic cat comes home to electricity, slinking past shifting deserts of meaning.

"The first rose is of granite. The second rose is of red wine. The third rose is of lark feathers. The fourth rose is of rust. The fifth rose is of longing. The sixth rose is of tin. But the seventh–the most delicate, the devout, the nocturnal, the sisterly–shall grow, immediately following your death, out of your tomb."

"Seven nights higher red migrates to red." Here is no halt for identities, only a blue recognition of distances beyond blue.

How time stands still for a thrower of shadows! How empty of doubt, the fullness of Adamic speech. . .

The purest coincidence of system & accident.

103

I place the ashen flower, its darkness
fully grown, under glass.
– Celan

Within my ashen masks
The lights are extinguished.
– Goll

The apprehension of voices in a darkened room. One word between them. The thing not signaled or hidden; neither feared nor received.

Deceleration is the way to beauty. As measures lengthen, the insufficiencies show their lacework, their oceanic openings.

Thus, "an owl in vestments of night" is called to brood the ovum of a dying soul; and "a late bird" carries, all summer long, "the ice-grain in its beak."

What writing erases: a man, standing "on the threshold of the withered hour," decides to enter, compelled by "the drums of the final hour."

Recto, a plaster bust of the poet reciting, *verso*, with an unreal "sister-mouth," an admonition to virtue.

The burn of whiteness / witness. The book a scene of heavy curtains, wind-inhabited.

The moon was hacked to bits
– Celan

The moon-axe
Sinks into my marrow
– Goll

Unhealed untreated. The spilled goblet, under the spell of lunar gravity, floats to the floor. An accident of the blood; the waters superimposed on purpose.

Man-made mother, eroded word: body peering through the body.

"Terminal olive tree, my skeleton rises out of the Asiatic wastes." The first book opens as song in the wasteland; the last one laments & accuses its maker. "The foreign heart is hung, phosphorescent, in my ribcage."

To come to the city of the abandoned body, the book to come. Or to "drink from wooden bowls the ashes of the fountains" of an unknown city. "How is it that I still live? Uncertain god, to prove you to yourself."

Violation of, as method: extinct voice in the cistern.

Being divided by itself alone. The theremin interprets: the sonic flowerfall of primes.

105

The suns of death are white
– Celan

a sacred dagger slashes our death-sun
– Goll

The crisis of the object creates an image without analogy. From reference to face to face: *between* will bind its twin, or twist detail to overarching feature.

Such words must turn inside out in order to stay the same.

"The cry, the human cry out of the lightless body that like a sacred dagger slashes our death-sun." Solar cry that according to Copernicus inhabits the center of every voice.

"The suns of death are white like the hair of our child, who climbs out of the flood as you pitch a tent upon the dunes. Our child, who brandishes the knife of happiness over us with extinguished eyes."

Mergence of crime & cry in "the crisis of the object." An emergency everlasting. Hands shy away from this immaculate damage; the same hands hover over the throat of the theremin.

Scratched-out script: bloodline of unstable constellations.

Black milk of early morning
– Celan

The red milk of strength
– Goll

The complete works: the crumpled plan.

The long breath brought to term.

"Woman, anti-woman, rise out of your occult prehistory to exert
your double dominion. . . Androgyne, solar moon....For the love
of nothing, in a card game pitting one against the other, marry and
betray the Ego-world."

"A grave in the winds...a grave in the clouds...play death more
sweetly...scrape the fiddles more darkly...then you will rise as
smoke...death is a master from Germany."

Each bell-howl, as skin-stretched-sky & industry.

Land peopled by pillars. Chorus, the irrevocable.

The white heart of our world
– Celan

to find the heart of the world
– Goll

Mazed interior. This curving wall has one side only.

Here, a calm contemplative terror is applied to patterns – to polyps whose tentacles are polyps with tentacles.

"Where water stirs, there night dives in, expecting to find the heart of the world."

"The sea's ink-blackness around the mouth....Brow that broods over shells and waves... beautiful, in place of the heart....O knocking, that comes and goes! In finitude undulate the veils."

What smoulders in the smallest cell: the groan of *against,* the shudder of great negation.

Answering quiet to send / uncanny echo to question.

NOTES ON CELAN'S *WEGGEBEIZT*

Susan Stewart

WEGGEBEIZT vom
Strahlenwind deiner Sprache
das bunte Gerede des An-
erlebten—das hundert-
züngige Mein—
gedicht, das Genicht.

Aus—
gewirbelt
frei
der Weg durch den menschen-
gestaltigen Schnee,
den Büßerschnee, zu
den gastlichen
Gletscherstuben und –tischen

Etched away by the
radiant wind of your speech,
the motley gossip of pseudo-
experience—the hundred—
tongued My—
poem, the Lie—noem

Whirl-
winded,
free
a path through human-
shaped snow,
through penitent cowl-ice, to
the glacier's
welcoming chambers and tables

Etched away from
the ray-shot wind of your language
the garish talk of rubbed-
off experience—the hundred
tongued pseudo—
poem, the noem.

Whirled clear
free
your way through the human-
shaped snow,
the penitents' snow, to
the hospitable
glacier rooms and tables.

Tief
in der Zeitenschrunde
beim
Wabeneis
wartet, ein Atemkristall,
dein unumstößliches
Zeugnis

Deep
in the time crevasse,
by
honey-comb ice
there waits, a Breathcrystal
your unannullable
witness.

—*trans. John Felstiner*

Deep
in Time's crevasse
by
the alveolate ice
waits, a crystal of breath,
your irreversible
witness.

—*trans. Michael Hamburger*

An encounter with Paul Celan's poems often raises the question of whether or not it is possible to translate them. In his introduction to his 1972 translation of a selection of the poet's early poems, Michael Hamburger says, "much of the later work is virtually untranslatable," though Hamburger eventually took up that task in a selected poems in 1980. John Felstiner's recent biography of Celan is an extended and profound meditation as well on the possibility of translating him—at one point Felstiner writes hopefully "his genius at uncalled-for repetition becomes a symptom proving that translation, a form of repetition, can indeed occur," and at another, "because we cannot translate *Ziv* [a word for the light in the Shechinah found in Gershom Scholem's *Von der mystischen Gestalt der Gottheit*], we must not." Felstiner also went on, in 2000, to publish a selected poems.

Yet perhaps instead of asking whether it is possible to translate Celan's work, we should first ask if it is ethical to translate his work—that is, ethical to resolve the poems into the fixed forms of new poems in other languages, for in many ways questions of what can and cannot be done in translation are not adequate to the problems of witnessing, facing, and addressing that Celan's work raises. Of course we can take our clue from the poet himself, whose lifelong project of translating poems and prose by Mandelstam, Blok, Dickinson, Shakespeare, Cioran, Esenin, Ungaretti, Apollinaire, Rimbaud, Valéry, Char, Michaux, and many others speaks to his regard for, and the hopes he placed in, translation. And we can argue for a literal translation that stays as close as possible to the meanings of individual words. But words live in speech as well as in language, and by insisting on a decontextualized German, by in many ways treating German as if it were a dead language, Celan forces us to read between the uncertain traces of etymology and the unheard resonances of the colloquial. Celan said in conversation "no one person is 'like' another...only distanced can my reader understand me…always grasping only the grilled bars between us." These "grills" can be seen to split words into morphemes and regroup them by force. Celan relies on condensation and displacement, neologism and historical resonance at once so that translation seems to have begun from the start—in composition.

Nevertheless, poems are not persons and whereas the linguistic capabilities of persons may seem to be able to transcend the differences between poems, it is not at all clear that similarities between poems can transcend the differences between persons and, specifically, that poems can remedy the problem of the unintelligibility of the expression of suffering even, or perhaps especially, when the expression of suffering is inseparable from the poet's intention. Behind Celan's comments on likeness, we can hear the imploring questions of *Lamentations* 2:13: "What shall I take to witness for thee? what shall I liken to thee…What shall I equal to thee, that I may comfort thee?"

The particularity of Celan's art demands an inexhaustible and universalizing labor of attention and semantic judgments, a task for the present and the future. But this very particularity demands that we also refuse all efforts to universalize or simulate his practice, or to merge the historical specificity of his referents with other historical terms. Two of the greatest torments of his post-war life— the ready adaptation of his "Todesfuge" by German audiences in the generations after the war and the false accusation of plagiarism brought against him by Claire Goll—are centered in the negation of individuality that joins too-ready appropriation and too-facile similarity. Doesn't seriously translating Celan's intention commit us to refusing the finitude of translations—to turn instead to the literal German words of his poems and books of poems and, whether we know no German or some or are native speakers, learn and re-learn the German he writes as a perpetually foreign language?

Perhaps the only way to approach Celan's work is to attempt to create a manifold reading that, as Felstiner indicates in his remarks on *Ziv*, does not forget the ever-present possibility of untranslatability and even invisibility and so constantly defers the creation of a new or substitute work. All translations of Celan's work can be brought under the consideration of an unfolding understanding that also leans against, continually comes back to rest upon, his inscribed German words. Looking at versions of "WEGGEBEIZT" by these two well-known translators of Celan, we can see some of the places in the German that resist translation, or open to it, or in various ways cause gaps or disparities.

Both Felstiner and Anne Carson, in her study *Economy of the Unlost,* discuss the importance of the initial capitalized word "WEGGEBEIZT" and its relation to acid techniques in printmaking and particularly in the work of the poet's wife, Gisèle Lestrange-Celan. Felstiner suggests that the poem "has a curative effect just by sharing in his wife's art." And Carson writes: "both etching and epigraphy are processes of excision which seek to construct a moment of attention by cutting away or eliding away what is irrelevant so as to leave a meaning exposed on the surface. Drastic negation is inherent in the physical act."[1] Yet once the translator makes a judgment to emphasize *beizen* in the opening *weggebeizt* as "etched," the word's secondary meaning in geological erosion is submerged. Reading *vom* as "by" or "from" in turn results in varied ideas of agency, and it is not clear if the wind is the bearer of radiance or the beneficiary of it—*Strahlen* also merges the largest scale of nature with that of human marks in that it can indicate radioactive rays or penciled rays, and *bunte* can mean "motley" or

---

1   John Felstiner, *Paul Celan: Poet, Survivor, Jew* (Yale University Press, 1995), p. 218; Anne Carson, *Economy of the Unlost* (Princeton University Press, 1999), p. 113.

"garish," but it also means "colorful," and is a word used in speaking of color printing. Later *wirbeln* will similarly have a visual effect in *gewirbelt*'s resonance to the whirled state of snowflakes, smoke, and drum-rolls released into the air.

The break after *Mein*—indicates that a noun will arrive on the next line and here the possessive is linked to *Meineid*, a perjury or false note. *Gedicht* would mean "poem," but suggests, with this hovering prefix, "Falsepoem," also thereby indicating the invisible echo *gedacht* (imaginary or made up) once we reach the interposition of *Genicht*—the "not poem," which both translators, though in different order, convey as the "noem." But does the neologism "noem" really carry over the subtle shift in perception that occurs at the line break and then continues in the unfolding sequence of sublimated words and echo effects?

In breaking off at *durch den Menschen*—"through the men," Celan evokes a letter he wrote to Margul-Sperber, "mensch during the Nazi-time seemed a rhymeless word calling for rhyme." (Felstiner, p. 192) He goes on to explain that Nazi guards called their Jewish prisoners "dogs" and their German shepherds "men." (Felstiner, p. 27) Celan often practices a reversal of letters that Felstiner calls an "inverse" translation. Earlier we could say that the opening *weggebeizt* has such a relation to *gebieten* (order or command as the inverse of erase) and here "menschen" finds a "rhyme" in [men]Schnee. Earlier *weg* indicated something disposable, thrown away, or erased, and these meanings now come into contrast with *Weg*, which Felstiner decides to translate as "path" and Hamburger as "way." Felstiner's version thereby carries slightly more strongly how *Weg* as a noun in Celan's work resonates to Heidegger's famous essay on the *Holzweg*—a timber-track or forest path. Such a path is a way to thought and poetry as "under way" toward truth in language. *Weg* as path and *weg* as wiped out become contrary referents to the same signs, as something with the authenticity of the possessive and first-hand earlier bore as well the inauthenticity of the fake or lie.

Snow in Celan has a complex resonance as early as his 1942/43 "Winter" ("it's falling, Mother, snow in the Ukraine"), written after he learned of his mother's murder by gunshot in the camp where she was imprisoned. It was a particularly cold winter, and in 1943 he changed the title of his poem "Mutter" to "Schwarze Flocken," evoking black or dark flakes that could refer to the descent of ash or snow alike. In "Mutter"/"Schwarze Flocken" Celan also wrote "autumn in its monkish cowl brought tidings my way," and both poems allude to a 16th c. German folk song, "The snow has fallen." (Felstiner, 18-19) The *Bußerschnee* are fields of clean glacial snow melted by the sun into single peaks that resemble figures wearing cowls. *Buß* indicates penitent or repentant, and hence "penitent's snow." In English these phenomena are called "sun cups." When Celan goes on to speak of *Wabeneis*, using another compound, he evokes a different geological formation—the thin dust film over snow found at high altitudes that is then melted by the sun into the shapes of polygons with clean hollows in the center. Again, two contrary images are presented—the peaked pristine landscapes of sun cups and the chiaroscuro surfaces of honeycomb snow formations. When Felstiner writes "the time crevasse," he indicates geological time, whereas Hamburger commits himself to the more symbolic and allegorical choice of "Time's crevasse" and ends up allegorizing the ice as well as "alveolate" ice. But *Wabe*/ honeycomb is already a metaphorical term, and we are thrown back to the initial image of *Sprache* as both the everyday speech that animates the fixity of language and the language that freezes the metaphors of everyday speech.

Atemkristall also resists singular reference. Celan composed, in tandem with his wife's work, a series of lyrics called *Atemkristall*, which he referred to as "a word to witness for us both...born from your etchings." The first poem of this group begins "Feel free to / regale me with snow," and Lestrange-Celan's engravings were made in fact in shades of white, black, and gray. "Atem" also signifies Celan's long-standing motif of the *pneuma* and *ruach* (Greek and Hebrew respectively for the spirit or breath). *Kristall* is as well metonymic, according to Felstiner, throughout Celan's work, to Kristallnacht, which Celan had glimpsed as he passed through Berlin on his way to France in 1938. In the early 1950's his poem *Kristall* yoked the crystal's perfection and solidity to the breakage of Nazi violence. Yet *Kristall* also recalls the basic difference between natural forms like waves and snow cups that are events in process (moving, freezing, thawing, shifting) and crystalline structures, where the form is inseparable from the persistence of the material.[2]

In his classic 1922 study of iconology, *Iconostasis*, Pavel Florensky wrote of engraving as a deliberative and rational practice. He suggested that engraving "manifests the intellectual construction of images from elements wholly unlike the elements in the object being depicted; i.e. from the rational intellect's combining of various affirmations and negations. The engraving is therefore a schematic image constructed on the axioms of logic (identity, contradiction, the excluded third, and so on); and, in this sense, engraving has a profound connection to German philosophy, for, in both, the essential and definitive act is the deductive determination of reality solely through the logic of affirmation and negation, a logic with neither sensuous nor spiritual connections—in short, the task in both is to

---

2   See Hans Jonas, *The Phenomenon of Life* (Evanston, Northwestern University Press, 2001 reprint), p. 77.

create everything from nothing."[3] Florensky goes on to point out that on a piece of paper, an ephemeral surface that is "crumpled or torn easily, absorbs water, burns instantly, grows moldy, cannot even be cleaned," lines appear that have been made on a "very hard surface, one attacked and torn and deeply cut by the engraver's sharp knife." Hence the hard engraved strokes constantly contradict the fragile printed surface. Furthermore, by "arbitrarily choosing a surface," he contends, the engraver works with individualism and freedom: "in proclaiming its own law, [the engraver] thinks it unnecessary to attend to that law whereby all things in creation become authentically real."[4]

"WEGGENBEIZT" as the "bitten away," that which cuts into surface by acid (*mordant*) to reveal negatively the underlying image or content, seems to rhyme inversely against the accumulating fixed structures of *Wabeneis* and crystals. And just as the engraver's lines are hollows made in a hard surface from which the crushed paper picks up the black ink, so does the glacier inversely plow its whiteness up and through the earth. Under the glacier and under the acid, too, "ground" awaits its figuration. Thus the initial term of the poem surely indicates an important context for the work; yet to emphasize the initial idea of the poem as central is to under-estimate much of the work of the poem in time.

To cut into matter is the inverse of to free, whirling, in the air. Perhaps under and over the inauthentic, the authentic is uncovered or takes shape. The black and white and gray imagery of the poem etches away colorful lies and deceptions on a field of white. The mother as source of life is associated with the frozen

---

3   Pavel Florensky, *Iconostasis*, trans. Donald Sheehan and Olga Andrejev. Crestwood, N.Y.: St. Vladimir's Seminary, 1996, pp. 106-107.

4   Florensky, p. 109.

snow that accompanied her death, yet human shapes begin to take form. The penitent's snow, like an engraving, and like the familiar profiles/ chalices gestalt, can be "read" as positive and negative, humanly inhabited and empty, space at once. Like a pocket of air trapped within a block of ice or the crevasses of an avalanche, a "breathcrystal" can hold a possibility of life—a fixed shape that is also immaterial and so cannot be obliterated; the breathcrystal emerges with the "breath turns" (*Atemwende), as Pierre Joris has translated this term, of the poetic line itself.

Nevertheless, such a redemptive reading of the work of acid in the poem depends upon our not hearing the "tief" sounds or motifs of the poem. We make snow angels and snow men (another image of menschen-gestaltigen Schnee) to convince ourselves of the relevance of the human figure to nature's blankest canvas; we carve snow huts and rooms to make a space of dwelling where there is none. The biting away of the plate is not a final state, but an intermediate one. Similarly, Celan steps his poem, suspending the certainty of nouns throughout. The lines of the poem are themselves like rays; their sources and referents are bedazzled by the unfolding language that conveys them and the clearest, most irrefutable, words are those of undefined process and relation. A witness in turn is irrefutable, unannullable, and irreversible because he or she attends and waits— there in the world of description rather than explanation. Can we, too, not attend this poem as a work that is "bitten away,"one that has not yet revealed its content? Sometimes the print-maker leaves a thin veil of ink over the plate, giving it what is called the "plate tone"— an ineffable veil over the image, a negative rhyme for the veil of snow.[5]

---

5   My thanks to Marjorie Perloff and Martha Collins for their suggestions regarding these brief notes; whatever errors I have made remain my own.

IN MEMORIAM PAUL CELAN

Edward Hirsch

Lay these words into the dead man's grave
next to the almonds and black cherries—
tiny skulls and flowering blood-drops, eyes,
and Thou, O bitterness that pillows his head.

Lay these words on the dead man's eyelids
like eyebrights, like medieval trumpet flowers
that will flourish, this time, in the shade.
Let the beheaded tulips glisten with rain.

Lay these words on his drowned eyelids
like coins or stars, ancillary eyes.
Canopy the swollen sky with sunspots
while thunder addresses the ground.

Syllable by syllable, clawed and handled,
the words have united in grief.
It is the ghostly hour of lamentation,
the void's turn, mournful and absolute.

Lay these words on the dead man's lips
like burning tongs, a tongue of flame.
A scouring eagle wheels and shrieks.
Let God pray to us for this man.

IN MEMORY OF PAUL ELUARD

Paul Celan

Put the words in the dead man's grave,
the words he spoke in order to live.
Cradle his head among them
let him feel
the tongues of longing,
the tongs.

Put the word on the dead man's eyelid,
the word he refused to speak
to the one who said "thou" to him,
the word
his heart's blood rushed past
when a hand bare as his own
knotted the one who said "thou" to him
into the trees of the future.

Put that word on his eyelid:
maybe
his eye, still blue,
takes on a second, stranger blue,
a second blue,
and the one who said "thou" to him
dreams with him: we.

translated from the German by David Young

from UNDER THE DOME: WALKS WITH PAUL CELAN

Jean Daive

No matter whom, no matter what, Paul Celan reads no matter where because the word drives him to memory and memory is the imaginary space where the legibility of the world is acted out.

At the end of his life he finds the North German vocabulary a more faithful mirror of his memory where a—wild—etymology forms with utmost acuity and violence.

A recollection: near Avenue Emile-Zola, Paul Celan looks for a grocery store. He buys a lightbulb that he puts in a huge netbag. Carrying the netted lightbulb he moves on with assurance. And the net hangs heavy.

The world is illegible and the matter of words engenders a structure: the poem. Vibration of sense used as energy.

Often a word is the starting point. As if a man come from the East could read the illegible world with a vocabulary most radically alien to him.

Great listening, great attention, but Paul Celan does not exclude loose language. What he lets loose within language?

He reads the newspapers, all of them, technical and scientific works, posters, catalogues, dictionaries and philosophy.

A recollection: Lesieur Oil.

He reads Rilke, Trakl, Kafka, Heidegger. Listens to

conversations, notes a word heard in a store, in the street. He reads
Meister Eckhart.

He reads no matter where. (Posters, the placard for Lesieur
Oil that moves by mounted on a van.) He focuses his mirror on
difference, opposition. The word, for a moment, fixes memory.

"A poet is a pirate," he says often.

He reads Margarete Susmann, her book on Kafka. He reads
Martin Buber. Manuals on driving trucks, cars. Traffic rules.

The matter of words. Words as matter. Distance within logic.

Coming back from London, Paul Celan tells me that he has
seen God under the door: "A ray of light in my hotel room."

I repeat to myself:

tagnächtlich
die Bärenpolka:

à perpétuité,
la polka-des-ours:

à vie,
la polka-des-ours:

jusquà la fin des jours,
la polka-des-ours:

Walking in the rue d'Ulm (in May '68) Paul Celan says to me: "Last night I heard something like distant cannons."

Reading the posters around the pool on the place du Luxembourg: "Only the One exists," "We are all German Jews," "Forbidden to forbid." Paul Celan has a mocking smile.

"The world is uninhabited," he says on the terrasse of the Panthéon, "the moon already is."

Avenue Emile-Zola: the empty apartment he has occupied for a week now. In the bathroom he bends over the tub, dips his left hand in the water: underwear floats up. Laundry. "You'll excuse my finishing the laundry?" With his smile.

In a gray coat he crosses the Place du Palais-Royal. He suddenly stops under the thick snow. He seems unsure which way to go. He turns his head and walks on. He will cross the Seine.

I am watching him. He does not see me.

Rue de Richelieu: "Friends are the first to turn on you, don't forget that," he tells me.

As for God, quoting Kafka: "Sometimes yes, sometimes no."

The Hôpital Psychiatrique. The long tables in the refectory of Sainte-Geneviève-des-Bois.

Games of relationship between Paul Celan, Joerg Ortner, me.

Which?

"I gave your book to Joerg Ortner to read, an Austrian painter," he says one evening. Later he [confides] tells me: "The Austrian painter I mentioned, whom I gave your book, very much liked *Décimale blanche*... right..."

Joerg Ortner's black hat. At the cemetery of Thiais. The day of Paul Celan's funeral.

Chapter of translations.

Apropos *Windgalle and Treckschuttenzeit.*
        contrevent   temps des coches d'eau

All words are composites. The second term the most important. The verb is tied to the second term. There is a vertical sense.

Paul Celan chews a word like a stone. All day long. There is word-energy in this. It all goes into the energy of the composite word. Here we have his biography.

Paul Celan invites the reader to travel inside the word (voyage, labyrinth).

On the one hand, the composite noun—on the other, the word is not named. Paul Celan does not name the word.

Morphology.

Paul Celan's joy on discovering a word — *Windgalle*. He burrows into words.

Is there somebody in the word?

The word is no more,
The world is no more (no stronger).

I have to carry you.

Absence of the verb: the verb is absorbed into the energy of the composite noun.

Morphology.

Paul Celan walks looking at the ground. Lifts his head to note certain places. Lifts his head, for example, by the Place des Patriarches and looks toward the Public Baths.

Recollection: Paul back from London. "I have seen God, I have heard God: a ray of light under the door of my hotel room." And later Paul recalls Kafka's formulation: "Sometimes God, sometimes nothing."

Eternity present in the rue d'Ulm. In his study. In the garden. Near the pool.

Eternity is gray (Paul Celan).

Eternity is useless. It is called the waystations of the century.

Paul walks with his hands crossed in back.

To recollect a Sunday we spent together. Took the bus as far as the Opéra. The Saint-Lazare area. The theater. Then went into a café where Paul notices a woman sitting among the crowd. Her face drawn. Pale. He falls back, as if frightened. Pushes me. We rush out. In the street he tells me, "Her face reminded me of a friend who died."

High alert during our encounters.

Paul staring at my tie.

The gray coat. The gray coat's presence. Ample. The London type.

High forehead and gray coat.

His watch. The importance of the watch.

I should talk of who was no longer Paul. Seeing him in the hospital. The long table of the refectory. Gisèle and I and a voluble Paul.

Paul's wife, Gisèle. And the twin rings on their fingers.

The psychiatric hospital of Sainte-Geneviève-des-Bois.

The refectory, the dormitory. Paul's.

The refectory, the halls, the white metal gurneys on wheels.

The wind, the wind, the kite.

The deer stew Paul treated me to after my poems were published in German in the Zurich journal.

La Chope. The thirst and appetite in the way he said this name. "Let's eat at La Chope," he'd say.

Basically he had no eyes for things. In the street, no eyes.

"Jean Daive, what is your task?" Question he asked me in the Rue Gay-Lussac, near the Geographic Institute. Silence. Long silence. We cross the street. We're on the other sidewalk. He puts his hands in his pockets. It is mild. Autumn. Yes. Autumn. "Your task, Jean Daive!"

I look at myself and within myself I look at Gisèle. I write this today. Gisèle.

There is no reply possible. I look at him sweetly, with great attention.

Rue d'Ulm as lair and landmark.

Side by side, translating "Strette" at the Royal Panthéon. On his right.

At Paul's burial, in the car. Gisèle's hand. Her ring.

Her moist eyes. Her lips. And in the crowd, tall, the man with the black hat: Joerg Ortner.

The laurel wreath. The funeral wreath, severe and perfect, brought from Vienna to Paris by Karl Demus (on his lap).

The brutal shock of his disappearance. I "see" the jump into the Seine. I can see it. And I see again his two hands stirring the soapy water in the tub Avenue Emile-Zola, with his laundry soaking beneath the tiles. With elegance and determination.

Empty space of the apartment. Empty place. Big bookcase. Empty.

A word while walking. At the crossing of Boulevard Saint-Germain and Boulevard Saint-Michel, going north. The crowd of May '68. Paul looks at faces he's never seen before. As if—this is implied—the crowd should be familiar, always the same.
—The've come out of their holes and don't know they can never go back.
—After the events?
—Yes, after.

What is this sudden remembrance of Paul, so intense that I dream, this Saturday, 25th of March 1989, of Gisèle. In front of this store. In the street. I look at her and she knows I'm going to ask her to tell me everything. (Which she has already.)

Paul Celan—his failed suicide in the small room of the Rue de Longchamp. The blood and Gisèle's composure. Paul's happiness Rue de Longchamp. Paul's frozen happiness there. The newspapers every day, the mail every day, the everyday unhappiness of Germany, him, Germany. Of Germany and German.

The German language lived in Paris. On an island basically and perhaps to be carried in a Great Open Book with Gisèle, and then without her.

Without ring.

The poem he writes in the street and then telephones to her from a public phonebooth.

I imagine the poems of *Sprachgitter* telephoned this way and written along the Seine.

That I absolutely could not speak had long made my life impossible when I met Paul Celan, who had written *Sprachgitter* (1959): a grid, language. Not of words or images, but gathering the world into a grid to elucidate it.

Two women (Greta and Olga) preceded and led me to his universe: one of difficult beauty, the other beautiful without strangeness. A third would come.

The game of translation makes a grid appear before my eyes. The way an innermost secret slowly comes, can come, to us.

How could a grid contain madness?

Impossible to articulate, an absence behind absence plunges me into a life—a non-life. Everything implies deduction, and the grid authoritatively puts it in place.

Language has dimmed like a light, and I am walking in the snow one January morning when I meet two women.

The grid holds suffering that will writhe in convulsion and drama.

How could a grid worry about the locus of a language it steeps in a final emulsion?

A syntax tormenting the narrative that words can never untangle.

There is always a story or an idea to tell. A story means progression, means torment.

A word turns like a sun. Mirrored fullness that blinds words.

Sitting on Paul's right, at a table in the Royal Panthéon. Silence. He looks at me, smiles:
—Would you translate me?
—You know very well that is difficult!
—I know it is difficult, but I will help you.
—Alright.

A little later, on Paul's right, at a table in the Royal Panthéon—the same one—we start working on translating "Strette."

—A word is a word and translating me means finding always the right word (apropos of the series of botanical terms: granulous, fibrous, stemmed, compact, racemose and radial, reniform, lamellate and palmate, porous, runcinate). Sometimes you have to let the sense drift. And right away you have to go back to the beginning, to the literal meaning: it's the right one.

At the crossing of Rue des Ecoles and Boulevard Saint-Michel, Paul Celan asks me:
—Have you thought of writing in another language?
—No. And you?
—Yes, sometimes in French…But it is not possible.
—Why?
He smiles.

Apropos the first two lines of "Strette:" *Verbracht ins / Gelände:* what he authorizes with a violent stroke across the paper becomes:

Dé – porté dans l'étendue.

—You sometimes have to shift the meaning of the stanza, but find its balance, he says.

A poetry born of illness.

Subjects and conversations: the scandal ("Todesfuge," "Death Fuge:" "I immediately became the target of the antisemites…no…I became the target of all of Germany")—nazism—deportation—the scandal: the plagiarism affair, how it wounded him: "It's a plot/conspiracy"—the carpenter Zimmer—Hölderlin's tower—intransigeance—guilt—friendship betrayed—Antschel, Ancel, Celan—the Neckar—work camps—the Bukovina—the plagiarism affair: "An outrage"—Auschwitz and poetry: "Man will continue to

talk, man will continue to bear witness with or without Adorno"—
the camp (two lines, the one on the left, the one on the right, and
changing lines)—public readings—Gisèle—Nicolas de Staël—
Giacometti ("Sometimes one has to be worldly like Giacometti")—
The *Ephémère*—André du Bouchet—Ezra Pound—the Kabbala—
Meister Eckhart—Rosa Luxemburg—Paris—the Seine—the
Contrescarpe—Walking in the Luxembourg Gardens—Rue de
Pot-de-Fer—Rue Tournefort (on the threshold his ritual formula: ("I
won't ask you in because my cleaning woman didn't come today")—
"I want to translate you: I want to translate *Décimal blanche*...
right"—Heidegger—Visiting me in Rue Coquillière: "This is a real
poet's place"—Rue de Longchamp—Berlin—Avenue Emile-Zola—
the Russian Revolution—Mandelstam—Peter Handke—Prague—
Hölderlin—Klaus Demus—Vienna—Tristan Tzara—May '68—We
are all German Jews—Nelly Sachs—Daniel Cohn-Bendit.

What is my recollection of Paul today, twenty years later?

And how did this immediate triangulation happen? Paul—
Gisèle—me.

There is much silence on this, much that remains unsaid. Even
today my mouth drops open.

Nevertheless many trips: London, Venice, Jerusalem,
Amsterdam, Antibes.

His meeting Martin Flinker on the Pont-Neuf. Paul became a
different man. Knowing everything about Germany and everybody.
Every writer and every publisher.

At a table in back, in the Greek restaurant in the Rue de l'Ecole-de-Médecine, Paul is writing in his notebook. A plate of tarama, paper, and fork. Writing, on a corner of the table. Cold and self-contained. He does not see me. Does not feel my presence. I leave.

The chestnut trees. Chestnuts. Light rain falling between us, between the leaves. He tells me he expects a telegram from Germany. Sadly, tiredly.

All that he does not tell me and all that I know from Gisèle. All the secret whispers of a man and a woman, transmitted secretly.

To describe his face: contorted—smiling—hurt—judgmental—sovereign—generous—nostalgic—imperious—contorted—luminous—childlike—severe.

Paul calls me. He has finished his translation of *Décimal blanche*. He worked during Christmas vacation. He wants me to clarify the meaning of certain words. He asks me to explain "voix pivotale," and finally "énoncé:"
—"What does "énoncé" mean?"
—The word will remain untranslated.

It is over this untranslated word that I meet Joerg Ortner, who asks me:
—What does "énoncé" mean?

We are meeting Place des Vosges. Paul Celan is dead.

We are working at his big table in Avenue Emile-Zola. He is

133

very concentrated, very precise. He loves words. He erases as if there should be blood.

The last phone call: his voice somber, tormented, hollow. It actually trembles, and I am filled with terror.

—Jean Daive, I don't see you any more. Why?

Almost sobbing. We talk. We must see each other. We make an appointment for Avenue Emile-Zola. Two days later, nothing. Nobody. Paul Celan has disappeared.

On Monday morning of April 20, 1970, Gisèle on the phone:

—Jean, did you see Paul on Sunday? No? I am worried. I'm without news. Paul has disappeared.

My distress afterward. That lasts and lasts. A whole month of emptiness, of anguish. Of lacking ground. Days of absolute emptiness. I feel his death as a break with the world of men. With language.

I can imagine the night, the Seine, the Mirabeau Bridge perhaps, no doubt (already named in his poems). A Sunday.

Then Gisèle. Day after day during the wait, the disappearance, the flight, the going away, the lack of signs.

Day after day. In tears, on my birthday. At the Vagenende. There and elsewhere. Lost in Paul's death.

One evening Gisèle says:

—I am going to the morgue to identify Paul.

The evening after:

—He was unrecognizable. The face puffed up and black.

And a little earlier:

—Jean, Paul's body has been fished out of the Seine. At the last sluice-gate.

While Paul is disappeared Gisèle tells me:

—Paul left his watch on his night table. Paul is dead.

—Ah? Why?

—Paul always kept his watch on his wrist. He told me: the day I take off my watch I'll have decided to die.

So Gisèle knew.

The Aegean is in front of me. Against my table and beyond my book, pines and waves breaking on the sand. The Aegean is a wound. I never talk of it. It is blue, transparent, I see it. I don't see the wound.

A man digs in front of a stone wall white as a sepulchre: it's a low house set deep in the ground, without window or door, and I can't help thinking of my father's vanishing.

I no longer know or simply don't know what vanished with him. But he left an infinite of presumptions and my mother's vengeance.

The island is still calm on this late afternoon. I watch a donkey immobile enough to disenchant the stone landscape.

Why bring the donkey into the wound? The island is calm and flat and silent and yet all I look at is convex. The donkey, the spade, the wave, the sepulchre, all these moments lived in and held against the sky come back to me whereas they should dig another vanishing.

I think of Paul Celan. I am in a beautiful house overlooking the blue sea. Ed listens as I tell her for the first time of my father. I think of Paul Celan. I am in a beautiful white house. I think of the books he gave me and the moments surrounding them, highly charged always. One of them comes back to me:

A golden light fills his office in the Rue d'Ulm. We have just had lunch. We are in a good mood.

—I am going to give you, he says, the *Sonnets* of Shakespeare that I have translated. I just received copies. They are love poems addressed probably—according to the specialists—to a young man he had loved....Read Sonnet LVII.

He is sitting at the table. He looks at me gravely. Inscribes the book.

[...]

March 1968. I remember. I was going to do some shopping with my netbag and cry under the paulownias. Impossible to be. Impossible to write. I was a brain-cry that could not be expressed. Some fragments got done which I showed to Paul at his request. ("You write, Jean Daive?—Yes—Show me!" Paul's tone authoritative, even imperious. I showed him. "I like very much how you write, Jean Daive. I would like to translate you some day and I'd like to translate these poems for a Swiss journal." Which he did.)

But I want to remember more precisely, juxtapose these two moments. March 1968. My absolute solitude and anxiety under the paulownias, the shopping bag, and one of our last walks, that is to say, an errand we did together Avenue Emile Zola. Paul very alone, bitter, I should think (sulfurous solitude), holding a large netbag into which he slips a lightbulb he has just bought.

[…]

A recollection of Gisèle's.
"One whole summer long I wanted to repaint the apartment in Rue de Longchamp… (she had kicked Paul out of this apartment in the 16th arrondissement and above all away from herself) and spending hours on the ladder, I wanted, really wanted to die."

Gisèle is a good storyteller. She has this in common with my mother as well as the same face. Bony, touching, tender, angular, skinny. Gisèle tells me of Paul's failed suicide, the maid's room where she discovered him.

The chestnut tree and the garden of my childhood. Then the chestnuts of the avenues. The leaves, the luminous green, the chestnuts in autumn. A green light above us, domed. Conversation and footsteps. Paul on my left.
—I'm expecting a telegram from Germany.
—Ah.
—I would like refuse going there.
—Ah.
—I would like to refuse going there.
—Ah.

[…]

Basically Paul's presence takes place under the sign of three women: Greta, Olga who makes me discover his work, and Gisèle who explains the man to me. An identical cluster passes through Greta, Gisèle, Paula. Olga is something else. She is a wife.

Greta in my arms in Vienna and in Paris. I think I am dreaming. A strange and seemingly paradoxical summer in my arms. She reads in the Bibliothèque Sainte-Geneviève. I read in the Bibliothèque nationale. I pick her up every day in the late afternoon. And repeatedly, mainly four times, our exchanges upset me. Greta asks:
—What are you reading these days?
—Proust.

A smile. The amused smile of a woman in the know. In the know for two. The first time I did not really understand. Even though I felt ill at ease.
—How strange…because we too have—our—Proust.
—Ah.
—Yes…Robert Musil. (This is in 1958.)

Time passes.
So a little later. Same Situation: Bibliothèque Sainte-Geneviève.

Same walk. Same café or even room.
—What are you reading these days?
—George Bataille.
—Who is that?

—A great contemporary philosopher.

A smile. I wait. And sure enough:
—How strange…because we too have a great contemporary philosopher.
—Ah.
—Yes…Ludwig Wittgenstein.

Time passes and the scene is not altogether the same. Greta knows I am disturbed and enthusiastic about Ponge. I am looking for first editions of Francis Ponge.
—So you are reading Ponge? (Amused smile.)
—Yes, I'm reading Ponge. He does laundry.
—Laundry?
—Yes, he cleanses the language, the words. And the dirty water is not without wit.
—Ah. (Greta saying Ah!)
A pause. Then:
—How strange…because we too have a poet who cleanses and scrubs spiritually.
—Ah.
—Paul Celan.

This is the first time I hear the name. And from lips I have been kissing.

In Paul Celan, spirituality is made of densities (structures of densities). The densities are superimposed. Their meanings are superimposed. In Ponge, there is cleansing. And the accumulated cleansings let spirituality appear from "the negative."

The reader is always free to reply: I understand what I am to understand.

Arcades of green light we walk under, often along the greenish surface of the Seine. Static glass and band of movement. Paul Celan:
—You are going to Prague?
—Yes!
—I'll give you a letter to take to a friend, Franz Wurm.

I am really going to Vienna to meet Greta, then to Prague with her.

Gisèle suspecting something and already waiting for the worst. Afterwards she tells me: I walked through Paris for hours and called out: Jean Daive.

Rue de Longchamp: bourgeois interior. Paul's large bookcase that he left there. In the other room which I don't see, a large round table a meter/yard from the double bed. The apartment has seen all of Germany in procession.

In Rue Cujas (we like this street and its corner bookstore), Greta says to me:
—But in Trakl there is in addition (compared to Paul Celan) the dimension of incest, which you should understand perfectly.

Basically, she knows nothing about me (1958).

Monologue. Selfportrait:
—I love four-fruit jam. Ah, yes…Cherries, strawberries, raspberries, currants…Robert Musil—Ludwig Wittgenstien—Georg

Trakl—Paul Celan.

Rue d'Ulm. Place de la Contrescarpe. Rue du Pot-de-Fer. Rue Tournefort. I accompany him to where some years later Edith is supposed to move "us." The same courtyard. The same (infernal) echo. The world amplified. A cave. Here Paul went out of his mind. Then the police take him to Sainte-Geneviève-des-Bois. A horror. A world out of the Middle Ages.

—Jean Daive, do you know what the nurse says when he comes into the dormitory in the morning:
"Up, you corpses!"

Somewhat later in our long conversation orchestrated masterfully by Paul, the virtuoso of themes, of memory (Tzara), of reading (Rilke, Trakl), of daily life (budding friendship among patients), he gives me a plaintive (seductive) look which is not really a reproach (forestalls it in fact):
—Last time you gave me a book: *Testament* by Roger Gilbert-Lecomte.
—Yes.
—I read it carefully.
—Yes.
—My doctor found me reading this book.
—Ah.
—It was a difficult moment for him and me. You are reading a book? he asks. Yes. He picks it up, closes it and reads the title. What? You read a book called *Testament!* How did this get in here? A present from a friend. The doctor leaves, after asking me to stop reading it.

I look at his laughing eyes, his smile. He is delighted to see my consternation.

Whenever I leave Sainte-Geneviève-des-Bois that I too experience as a prison house, a feeling of freedom washes over me. Between the road and the hospital, a peaceful space, a meadow slopes toward an absence of walls. When I point this out to him:
—No more need for walls, no more need for barbed wire as in the concentration camps. The incarceration is chemical. The prisoner is chemical: he cannot take two steps on his own. But he can look at the outside. He can talk, right…

There is no color in Paul's books (he also never wears colors). But there are all the nuances of white, black, gray.
—Pigeon gray—Paris gray, he says.

Walking on Rue d'Ulm, by the Cinematheque, he seems to be fighting with himself, his two hands out in front of him, menacing, convulsive, his fingers snapping in the air. Fingers with black nails. Earth under them.

I often see his nails with the earth under them, as if he were burying, unburying, digging. Struggle with the real? Struggle with the dream of language?

The Place de la Contrescarpe with its paulownias resembles a small village, and he likes the sense of protection this hill gives him.

I see myself again at Sainte-Geneviève-des-Bois. As I enter the space splits in two. On my left a blinding lamp, on the right a butcher's cart piled with saws. At the same time I enter a space I know from childhood. Stone steps plunge toward the cellar: on the left coal, on the right potatoes. In the middle, in my father's arms, me with bleeding ear and gums. Paul Celan is waiting for me in front of a refectory table.

We're in autumn.

Against the wooden stairs, against judgment, Paul braces himself, opens his eyes: sometimes his glance seems to listen.

Sometimes moving forward in the air, searching for air, I find an autum, gold, impenetrable, what no word can unveil.

I understand: painted angels no longer guard the black holes.

The Contrescarpe as a choked garden. Behind a palissade, clochards are tossing empty bottles about that explode in the grass.

We watch.

Gisèle Celan has just told me that Paul has disappeared. Her voice anguished, extreme. She wants to see me, talk to me, tell me, explain.

"Narration torments the syntax." Alain Veinstein comes to see me on Place Saint-Sulpice where I reread the articles of the *Dictionary of Contemporary Works*. He comes to pick up his manuscript, "Giornata," which is under consideration at Mercure de France. He notices my anxiety:
—What's wrong?
—Paul Celan has disappeared.

Silence.
—Is there something I can do?

It is autumn. The voices in the street sound golden, float on the air. We walk. An autumn leaving a chestnut-lined avenue. We cross the Place des Patriarches. He looks toward the Public Baths.

He looks at me, smiles. We both smile.
—What's today's laundry, Jean Daive?
—Is there anything left to launder?

We go back up the Rue Mouffetard to 45 Rue d'Ulm. His office. He opens the dark blue folder with poems by Klaus Demus.

We work all Sunday.

A buzzing all around, sounds blending into the space. His steps enter like a legend, lithe.

I may know that our travels on earth are a dream. They must be. Interrupted by the flash of an encounter.

We walk by the chestnut trees. A bleached out space. Rotten pavement. He walks. I walk. Late afternoon. He is trembling or, more exactly, a strange stubborn silence makes him gloomy. He wants to talk, his lips are trembling, as are his hands. He looks at me. Opens his mouth. Nothing. We walk on. Rue Gay-Lussac. A bus stop. He holds out his hand, painfully.
—Pardon me, Jean Daive. I'll take the bus.

There is a transition from the chestnut trees of the child who

144

counts the leaves to those of the walker who counts chestnuts.

Water, the carafe of water, because he is thirsty.

The impenetrable—inhuman—distance between him and the Other. A distance where the remains of the world may accumulate: I mean the remains.

On his finger, his ring.

Bizarre references in conversation:
—Nowadays, Jean Daive, it takes 1500 francs to buy a pair of shoes (1969).
—Ah.

Truth does not like powder, does not look for powder. Yet that day snow falls on us. Enormous flakes thicken the space. And the world turned opaque becomes hard, impossible to interpret.
—Can you see in this, he asks, the ground is dangerously slippery.

I briskly take his arm. He is slipping. He prepares to slip and in falling reads the advertisement on a passing van:
—Lesieur oil. Ha! Ha! That's too funny!
I hold his arm firmly.

The man: seduction and the neutral—the charm of a distance.

Walking can make the change of place euphoric. A step. A step and another step. A step. I walk. I go. I can plunge my steps into gloom: but the steps break the anxiety, overheat the distance within.

Cosmic dust covers us. The wind lifts the air.

—I'm writing like never before, he says.

Astonished to be writing. Most often astonished not to be writing.

Each day, its astonishment.

Autumn made of cranes and cables: geometric tunes around the sky, and us there, askew, explosives double-charged with pallor and stubborn silence, we move on, but—how to put it?—without dodging (I insist), without fail (I insist). So all must be said and all will be said. Without sham (I insist).

[...]

A question comes up after all. When I told him that I wanted to start a magazine, why did he say: I'll give you something. And why—this is the real question—did he give mes these two poems: "Les Bains-Douches" and "L'Or"? (The word Bains-Douches supposedly "implicit"—always at a distance.)

And why did he translate those particular five poems of mine for the *Gazette de Zürich*? Interesting, i.e. turbulent, but perhaps without real strength. No doubt I offered an Openness where Paul mirrored himself. A credible—different—Open: the authentication of poetry:

—You like Rilke?

—Like Rilke! The Open...

—Yes, the Open... he concludes.

There is a trap. There is a trap between Paul and me. And the trap seems necessarily to go on and repeat itself (What did Gisèle tell you? You've seen Gisèle, haven't you? Call her! Go see her!) Between Paul, me and Gisèle. I am aware that I put myself between him and her, and aware of my power to move/shift the trap.

[…]

I see again his burial. I imagine his body in the coffin. He sees. Our looking. Her looking—through tears. Her nose, in the car, straight, slim, outlined against the air. She gives off, carries a scent. And him still there. He looks. He looks. My gums are bleeding. Nothing will stop. Of course. He looks. Damp passion, moist lips.

I would like to oppose, no, juxtapose, no, pose apprenticeship and writing.

I say no. That's not the problem. Of course we have to learn, but learn orality (after Paula) at the expense (I insist) of poetry.

What is it (poetry)? And what is it in the arms of X. or Greta? A bomb, no?

Something (in words) is a prayer. Often. No, not prayer but spoken: *parole*. An oral spirituality or flash, star, flare.

Metaphor—but real. Lived.

I see again Greta walking in front of me in the snow, in Vienna, and between us we are happy to carry the Christmas tree.

Paul was there.

Greta.

The child, a Christmas tree with candles, snow, silver balls, angel hair—and us.

Greta in boots. Knotty knees and knotted, but vertiginous sex.

On the edge of the bed. Red legs.

How to love, and then how to talk? I mean, we slide: the space allots us a word. Our roles seem more complicated for being masked.

I come to this (terrible and unarticulated) perception while translating first by myself then beside him "Engführung."

I translate by myself (without understanding all) "Engführung." Why this poem? Why request this one? He seems to make me decipher a possible ars poetica for the end of time.

The mother carries the child. The whitewashed arches form a white moon. I cry. The child's ear is bleeding.

Again the elder trees. Again the bleeding gums. Red and red blood.

In the shade of the walnut tree, as a child. Deep in the garden. I know I was waiting.

The dream. The hand in the dream. The water in the dream.

The bedroom in the dream. I mean: I know I was waiting for what adults forget.

The royal step:
—Poetry, Jean Daive, poetry!

One evening on Boulevard Saint-Michel, some years after Paul's death, Joerg Ortner turns the pages of a book he has found. He shows me the grandiose places where Rilke lived. The relation between the poet and his space is everything. In fact, the poet writes. He is a bit of straw in the black fever of the room he occupies.

Paul, the nightowl.

What does he do at midnight in Rue Tournefort, at the bottom of that buzzing courtyard?

One day I dropped a spoon in this courtyard of Rue Tournefort: the echo of its fall still sounds in my ears. A loud crash. Persistent vibrations from those walls.

He is sensitive to red threads, to designation. I designated him, sent him the manuscript of *Décimale blanche.* He did not respond.

All these years (1965-1970) seemed an eternity fusing psalms and sloshing noises.

The Contrescarpe is the place that welcomes the young poet. ("I salute the paulownias"). Paris, that is, the Contrescarpe.

The air tastes of powder and the ear picks up wind rustling

in the leaves of our chestnut trees. We have taken refuge behind the trunks I am counting. We talk. He talks:

—Use the colon. It syncopates.

—There is no colon that saves…

—…saves?

—…meaning, for example.

—Give me an example.

—I take as example: "Einmal"…you see?

—I see…

—Put a colon before the second line: you'll save a therefore.

—So a colon for *da.*

—A colon for *da.*

—Fine…But for *ichten* (in *gedicht* and *genicht*), *vernichtet* for example. You would put a colon for…

—No colon…You have to translate.

—And when you don't have to translate you put a colon…

Paul smiles. And continues:

—It is not always possible to shift the colon onto the meaning.

—I love hearing you say it.

—For *vernichtet, ichten,* I suggest for example: *anéanti, néanti.*

He again smiles. Our tensions—we are tense—are slight. He looks at the chestnut trees. I smile at him. My book-keeping is exasperated. We have come to a stop. He stopped in order to talk to me. We are face to face. This moment of waiting exasperates me. Because it's a checkmark. And I don't overly like checked conversation—*travelling*—standing still in the dust whose ground and smell change from one moment to the next. And I imagine the color changing with the conversation. (I have experienced such with Alain Veinstein, Claude Royet-Journoud, and Ortner who managed to keep me standing for 180 minutes = telling me over 3 long hours the history of the wall and fresco in the Luxembourg.)

"We must wash Rimbaud's heart." (Joerg Ortner)

Elements of destruction, of the city destroyed during May '68. Gun-fire. Gas. Bombs. Paving stones. Burned cars. Helmets. Barricades. Trees knocked down.

—This isn't the moment to rewatch *Battleship Potemkin*...says Paul.

—"They" would not understand your humor.

We're leaving the Ecole and turn to the right.

Sometimes his presence, our conversation echo like an aquarium or hothouse. We feel suffocated. He knows all the plants. And later in the night, G. knows all about the sexuality of fish.

It is raining. The mirrors are shrouded. Who is the dead sister?

—I am going to see an aunt in London, he says.

Salty saliva.

When he shakes my hand he must sense an obscure grief in me and a child's stammer.

He wants to calm, veil, explain while I know his darkness.

The first seconds are a flash of lightning, that fast. The torment turns, and our pain slides off. We can talk to each other.

—So?...

—You brought me your poems?

—Bah…
—Show them to me!
—You know…
—Yes, I know… We'll go eat at La Chope afterwards.

One afternoon he lets me read "Du liegst." He explains the
sieve and the sow. The murders. Rosa Luxemburg. The Eden hotel.

He evokes Berlin. His voice warm and as if muted. It no
longer sounds the universe. The man turns into the child who
suddenly among ruins does not understand the ruin of wars.
—And I have written this poem…right?...

He speaks to me at length about the murder of Rosa
Luxemburg and Karl Liebknecht, and with the same intensity as
when he speaks of his parents shot in the concentration camp.

Orgasm and full moon. Shortly after, dinner downstairs. White
tablecloth. Lit candles.
—There is no dessert tonight.
—But there never was…

The living room of the big house is white, the Aegean Sea,
blue. From my armchair I watch the configurations of the light
against the sky. Not quite labyrinthine. The mind does not multiply.
The mind does no damage. But I am drifting off. If I threw a stone I
would become a wound. No…because, to reach the deep, sensitive
eyes see nine different methods to compose a wound.

I look at the sea and at the rambler behind me, its red roses. I
look at the sea turned granite by the wind. The wind is blowing.

The sepulchre is open, the palm tree is open, the meadow is open. The man digs. The stone wall reaches up to the sanctuary.

The donkey immobile in the meadow's memory does not disturb the end of time.

Before me the open sea, and my thinking slowly comes ajar. I do not want to fall out of the sky. I do not want to fall into the deep. I am not a stone. I am only a wound. The chair and the rambler guard me.

In the cool of the white living room I wonder if there is a rite of passage and if Paul Celan's plunge into the Seine holds the idea of crossing a threshold. It is because the sky/heaven? no longer opens to man that man plunges into the waters and digs into the earth. Here too diverse methods compose an evaporation.

The deep is open.

One whole summer long I look at a donkey standing in his meadow. The meadow by the sea. The immobile donkey looks out, and I think he looks at a kind of stupor beyond time that conveys sainthood.

The meadow is at the end of the village, at the end of the island. Up against the sea. The donkey seems to wait. Humility is certainly a threshold or an absolute dissolution whose space remains to be occupied and experienced. The world of things assembles with the meadow, the sea, and the trees a geometric architecture. Time no longer added to anything.

153

Neither to time nor to warm chestnuts.

In Rue de Longchamp I look at Paul's bookcase he left behind.

One day I talk to him of his library left in Rue de Longchamp.
—Yes, I miss it. I am deprived of it, have cheated myself
out of it. You know, I had found *Le Grand Jeu* at a bouquinist's for
nothing. I'll give it to you. I'll tell Gisèle to give it to you. I have
found marvels…Paul Eluard, Baudelaire, Tzara, Picabia…

Gisèle gives me the 1948 Vienna edition of *Der Sand aus den
Urnen,* a book in three parts. The second part has always puzzled me:
    "Mohn und Gedächtnis," as if memory were not captive/a
slave to some poppy of the spirit.

Green branches and paved street. Gently, the humidity forms
beads. Hands behind his back, thoughtful. Face bowed. He can
silence the lament even if we are its backbone.

translated from the French by Rosmarie Waldrop

154

TRAVEL PAPERS

Carolyn Forché

> *Au silence de celle qui laisse rêveur.*
> —Rene Char

By boat to Seurasaari where
the small fish were called *vendace.*
A man blew a horn of birchwood
toward the nightless sea.

Still voice. Fire that is no fire.
Ahead years unknown to be lived—

*

Bells from the tower in the all-at-once, then
one by one, hours. Outside
(so fleetingly) ourselves—

In a still mirror, in a blue *within*
where this earthly journey dreaming
itself begins,

thought into being from the hidden to the end of the visible.

*

Mountains before and behind,
heather and lichen, yarrow, gorse,
then a sea village of chartreuse fronds.

Spent fuel, burnt
wind, mute swans.

*

We drove the birch-lined
highway from Dresden
to Berlin behind armored
cars in late afternoon,
nineteenth of June, passing
the black cloud of a freight
truck from Budapest.

Through disappearing
villages, past horses grazing vanished fields.

*

The year before you died, America
went to war again on the other
side of the world.
This is how the earth becomes,
you said, a *grotto of skeletons.*

*

In the ruins of a station: a soaked
bed, broken chairs, a dead coal-stove.

White weather, chalk and basalt,

puffins, fuchsia and history shot
through with particles
of recognition: this one
wetted down with petrol then
set alight, that one taking
forty rounds, this other
found eleven years later in a bog.

In the station house, imaginary
maps, smoke chased by wind, a registry
of arrivals, the logs of ghost
ships and a few prison
diaries written on tissue paper.

*

Do you remember the blue-leaved lilies?
The grotto, the hoar-frost, the frieze?

Through the casements of glass hand-blown
before the war, a birch tree lets snow drop
through its limbs onto other birches. Birch twigs
in wind through glass.

Who were we then? Such
a laughter as morning peeled
its light from us!

*

You said the cemeteries were full in a voice

like wind plaiting willows—fields in bloom
but silent with no grasshoppers or bees.
What do you want then? You with your

neverness, your unknown,
your book of things, you
with years once ahead to be lived.

*

Your father believes he took you
with him, that you are
in the urn beside your sleeping mother,
but I am still writing with your hand,
as you stand in your still-there of lighted words.

*

Such is the piano's sadness
and the rifle's moonlight.
Stairwells remember,
and also doors, but windows do not—

do not, upon waking, gaze out a window
if you wish to remember your dream

*

This ache of hope that you will come back—
the cawing flock is not your coming.

Did you float toward Salzburg? As a wind
in the mustard fields?— or walk instead
beside yourself through the asylum in Krakow?
Hours after your death you seemed
everywhere at once like the swifts at twilight.
Now your moments are clouds
in a photograph of swifts.

*

In the hour held
open between day and night
under the meteor showers of Perseid
we held each other for the last time.

Dead, you whispered *where is the road?*

There, through the last of the sentences, just there—
through the last of the sentences, the road—

from SHIBBOLETH: FOR PAUL CELAN

Jacques Derrida

III.

Let us remain for the moment with the dates that we recognize through the language-grid of the calendar: the day, the month, and sometimes the year.

First case: a date relates to an event that, at least *in appearance and outwardly*, is distinct from the actual writing of the poem and the moment of its signing. The metonymy of the date (a date is always also a metonymy) designates part of an event or a sequence of events in order to recall the whole. The mention "13th of February" forms a part of what happened on that day, only a part, but it stands for the whole in a given context. What happened on that day, in the first case we are going to consider, is not, in appearance and outwardly, the advent of the poem.

The example is that of the first line of "In eins" ("As One"). It begins with "Dreizehnter Feber," "Thirteenth of February."

What is gathered and commemorated, in a single poetic stroke, in the unique time of this "In eins"? And is it a matter of one commemoration? The "as one," all at once, several times at the same time, seems to constellate in the uniqueness of a date. But this date, in being unique and *the only one*, all alone, the one of its kind—is it one?

And what if there were more than one thirteenth of February?

Not only because the thirteenth of February recurs, becoming each year its own revenant, but above all because a multiplicity of events, in dispersed places—for example, on a political map of Europe, at different epochs, in foreign idioms, may have come together at the heart of the same anniversary.

IN EINS	AS ONE
Dreizehnter Feber. Im Herzmund	Thirteenth of February. In the heart's mouth
erwachtes Schibboleth. Mit dir,	An awakened shibboleth. With you,
Peuple	Peuple
de Paris. *No pasarán.*	de Paris. *No pasarán.*

Like the rest of the poem, and well beyond what I could say concerning them, these first lines seem *evidently* ciphered.

Ciphered, evidently, they are: in several senses and in several languages.

Ciphered, first of all, in that they include a cipher, a number, the cipher of the number thirteen. This is one of those numbers in which randomness and necessity cross, in order to be consigned at a single time. Within its strictures, a ligament binds together, in a manner at once significant and insignificant, fatality and its opposite: chance and coming-due [*chance et échéance*], coincidence in the case, that which *falls*—well or ill—together.

DIE ZAHLEN, im Bund	THE NUMBERS, bonded
mit der Blider Verhängnis	with the images' doom
und Gegen-	and their counter-
verbängnis.	doom.

Und Zahlen waren	And numbers were
mitverwoben in das	interwoven into the
Unzählbare. Eins und Tausend...	innumerable. One and a thousand...

Even before the number 13, the *one* of the title "In eins" announces the con-signing and co-signing of a multiple singularity. From the title and the incipit onward, the cipher, like the date, is incorporated in the poem. They give access to the poem that they are, but a ciphered access.

These first lines are ciphered in another sense: more than others, they are untranslatable. I am not thinking here of all the poetic challenges with which this great poet-translator confronts poet-translators. No, I will limit myself here to the aporia (to the barred passage, *no pasarán*: this is what *aporia* means). What seems to bar the passage of translation is the multiplicity of languages in the same poem, at once. Four languages, like a series of proper names and dated signatures, like the face of a seal.

Like the title and the date, the incipit is read in German. But with the second line, a second language, an apparently Hebrew word, arises in the "heart's mouth": *shibboleth.*

Dreizehnter Feber. Im Herzmund
erwachtes Schibboleth. Mit dir,

Thirteenth of February. In the heart's mouth
an awakened shibboleth. With you,

This second language could well be a first language, the language of the morning, the language of origin speaking of the heart, from the heart and from the East. "Language" in Hebrew is "lip," rather than "tongue," and does not Celan elsewhere (we will come to it) call words circumcised, as one speaks of the "circumcised heart"? For the moment, let this be. *Shibboleth*, this word I have called Hebrew, is found, as you know, in a whole family of languages: Phoenician, Judeo-Aramaic, Syriac. It is traversed by a multiplicity of meanings: river, stream, ear of grain, olive-twig. But beyond these meanings, it has acquired the value of a password. It was used during or after war, at the crossing of a border under watch.

The meaning of the word was less important than the way in which it was pronounced. The relation to the meaning or to the thing was suspended, neutralized, bracketed: the opposite, one might say, of a phenomenological *epochē* which preserves, first of all, the meaning. The Ephraimites had been defeated by the army of Jephthah; in order to keep their soldiers from escaping across the river (*shibboleth* also means "river," of course, but that is not necessarily the reason it was chosen), each person was required to say *shibboleth*. Now the Ephraimites were known for their inability to pronounce correctly the *shi* of *shibboleth*, which became for them, in consequence, *an unpronounceable name*. They said *sibboleth*, and, at that invisible border between *shi* and *si*, betrayed themselves to the sentinel at the risk of their life. They betrayed their difference by showing themselves indifferent to the diacritical difference between *shi* and *si*; they marked themselves with their inability to re-mark a mark thus coded.

This came to pass at the border of the Jordan. Another border, another barred passage, in the fourth language of the strophe: *no pasarán*. February 1936: the electoral victory of the *Frente Popular*, the eve of civil war. *No pasarán*: la Pasionaria, the no to Franco, to the Phalange supported by Mussolini's troops and Hitler's Condor Legion. Rallying cry or sign, clamor and banners during the siege of Madrid, three years later, *no pasarán* was a *shibboleth* for the Republican people, for their allies, for the International Brigades. What passed this cry, what came to pass despite it, was the Second World War, with its exterminations. A repetition of the First World War, certainly, but also of the dress rehearsal [*répétition générale*], its own future anterior, that was the Spanish Civil War. Dated structure of the dress rehearsal: everything happens [*se passé*] as if the Second World War had already begun in February of 1936, in a slaughter at once civil and international, violating or reclosing the

163

borders, leaving ever so many scars in the body of a single country—grievous figure of a metonymy. Spanish is allotted to the central strophe, which transcribes, in sum, a kind of Spanish *shibboleth*, a password, not a word in passing, but a silent word transmitted like a *symbolon* or handclasp, a rallying cipher, a sign of membership and political watchword.

> er sprach
> uns das Wort in die Hand, das wir brauchten, es war
> Hirten-Spanisch, ...
>
> im Eislicht des Kreuzers "Aurora" ...
> into our hands
>
> he spoke the word that we needed, it was
> shepherd-Spanish, ...
>
> in icelight of the cruiser "Aurora" ...

Amidst the German, the Hebrew, and the Spanish, there is, in French, the Peuple de Paris:

Mit dir,	With you
Peuple	Peuple
de Paris. *No pasarán.*	de Paris. *No pasarán.*

It is not written in italics, no more than is *shibboleth*. The italics are reserved for *No pasarán* and the last line, *Friede den Hütten*!, "Peace to the cottages!," whose terrible irony must surely aim at someone.

The multiplicity of languages may concelebrate, *all at once*, on the same date, the poetic and political anniversary of singular events, spread like stars over the map of Europe, and henceforth conjoined by a secret affinity: the fall of Vienna and the fall of Madrid, for, as we shall see, Vienna and Madrid are associated in one same line in another poem, entitled "Schibboleth"; once again memories of February, the beginnings of the October Revolution with the incidents linked to the cruiser *Aurora* and to Petrograd, both named in the poem, and even to the Peter and Paul Fortress. It is the last stanza of "In eins" that recalls other "unforgotten" singularities, that of "Tuscan," for example, which I will not here undertake to decipher.

"Aurora":	"Aurora":
die Bruderhind, winkend mit der	the brotherly hand, waving with
von den wortgroßen Augen	the blindfold removed from
genommenen Binde—Petropolis, der	his word-wide eyes—Petropolis, the
Unvergessenen Wanderstadt lag	roving city of those unforgotten,
auch dir toskanisch zu Herzen.	was Tuscanly close to your heart also.

| *Friede den Hütten!* | *Peace to the cottages!* |

But already within the hearth of a single language, for example French, a discontinuous swarm of events may be commemorated all at once, *at the same date*, which consequently takes on the strange, coincident, *unheimlich* dimensions of a cryptic predestination.

The date itself resembles a *shibboleth*. It gives ciphered access to this collocation, to this secret configuration of places for memory.

The series thus constellated becomes all the more ample and numerous insofar as the date remains relatively indeterminate. If Celan does not specify the day (13) and says only "February," ("Februar," this time and not *Feber*), as in the poem entitled

165

"Schibboleth," the memories of the same kind of demonstrations, with the same political significance, multiply: these brought together the People of Paris, that is, the people of the left, in the élan of a single impulse to proclaim, like the Republicans of Madrid, *No pasarán.* A single example: on February 12, 1934, after the failure of the attempt to form a Common Front of the Right, with Doriot, after the riot of February 6, a huge march took place, bringing together the masses and the leadership of the parties of the left. This was the origin of the Popular Front.

But if, in "In eins," Celan specifies the 13th of February (*Dreizehnter Feber*), one may think of February 13, 1962. I hand this hypothesis over to those who may know something about or can bear witness to the "external" date of the poem; I am unaware of it, but should my hypothesis be factually false, it would still designate the power of those dates to come, toward which, Celan says, we transcribe ourselves. A date always remains a sort of *hypothesis,* the support for a, by definition, unlimited number of projections of memory. The slightest indetermination (the day and the month without the year, for example) increases these chances, and the chances for the future anterior. The date is a future anterior; it gives the time one assigns to anniversaries to come. Thus on the 13th of February, 1962, Celan was in Paris. *Die Niemandsrose*, the collection in which "In eins" appears, was not published until 1963. Yet in moving from "Schibboleth," published eight years before, to "In eins," Celan specifies *13th* of February" where the earlier poem said only *February.* Thus something must have happened. February 13, 1962 was in Paris the day of the funeral for the victims of th massacre at the metro station Charonne, and of an anti-OAS demonstration at the end of the Algerian war. Several hundred thousand Parisians, the People of Paris, were marching. Two days later, the meetings that led to the Evian accords would begin. These

People of Paris remain those of the Commune, with whom one must band together: with you, Peuple de Paris. In the same event, at the same date, national war *and* civil war, the end of one and the beginning—*as* the beginning—of the other.

Like the date, *shibboleth* is marked several times, several times in *en une seule fois, in eins,* at once [in English and in the original]. A marked but also a marking multiplicity.

On the one hand, indeed, within the poem it names, as is evident, the password or rallying cry, a right of access or sign of membership in all the political situations along the historical borders *configured* by the poem. The *visa*, it will be said, is the *shibboleth*; it determines a theme, a meaning, or a content.

But on the other hand, as cryptic or numerical cipher, *shibboleth* also spells the anniversary date's singular power of gathering together. This anniversary date gives access to the memory of the date, to its proper to-come, but also to the poem—itself. *Shibboleth* is the *shibboleth* for the right to the poem that calls itself a *shibboleth*, its proper *shibboleth* at the very instant that it commemorates others. *Shibboleth* is its title, whether or not it appears in that place, as in one of these two poems.

This does not mean—two things.

On the one hand, this does not mean that the events commemorated in this fantastic constellation are non-poetic events, suddenly transfigured by an incantation. No, I believe that for Celan the signifying conjunction of all these dramas and historical actors will have *constituted* the signature of a poem, its signed dating.

Nor does it mean, on the other hand, that to have the *shibboleth* at one's disposal effaces the cipher, gives the key to the crypt, and ensures the transparency of meaning. The crypt remains, the *shibboleth* remains secret, the passage uncertain, and the poem unveils a secret only to confirm that there is something secret there, withdrawn, forever beyond the reach of hermeneutic exhaustion. A nonhermetic secret, it remains, and the date with it, heterogeneous to all interpretative totalization, eradicating the hermeneutic principle. There is no one meaning, as soon as there is date and *shibboleth*, no longer a sole originary meaning.

A *shibboleth*, the word *shibboleth*, if it is one, names, in the broadest extension of its generality or its usage, every insignificant, arbitrary mark, for example the phonemic difference between *shi* and *si* when that difference becomes discriminative, decisive, and divisive. The difference has no meaning in and of itself, but it becomes what one must know how to recognize and above all to mark if one is to make the step, to step across the border of a place or the threshold of a poem, to see oneself granted the right of asylum or the legitimate habitation of a language. So as no longer to be outside the law. And to inhabit a language, one must already have a *shibboleth* at one's disposal: not only understand the meaning of the word, not only *know* this meaning or *know* how a word *should* be pronounced (the difference of *h,* or *sh,* between *shi* and *si*: this the Ephraimites knew), but *be able* to say it as one ought, as one must be able to say it. It is not enough to know the difference; one must be capable of it, must be able to do it, or know how to do it—and here *doing* means *marking*. This differential mark that it is not enough to know like a theorem—that is the secret. A secret without secrecy. The right to alliance involves no hidden secret, no meaning concealed in a crypt.

In the word, the difference between *shi* and *si* has no meaning. But it is the ciphered mark which one must *be able to partake of* with the other, and this differential power must be inscribed in oneself, that is, in one's own body as much as in the body of one's own language, the one to the same extent as the other. This inscription of difference in the body (e.g., the phonatory aptitude to pronounce this or that) is nonetheless not natural; it is in no way an innate, organic faculty. Its very origin presupposes belonging to a cultural and linguistic community, to a milieu of apprenticeship, in sum, an alliance.

Shibboleth does not cipher something. It is not only a cipher, and the cipher of the poem; it is now, emerging from the outside-of-meaning where it holds itself in reserve, the cipher *of* the cipher, the ciphered manifestation of the cipher as such. And when a cipher shows itself for what it is, that is to say, in encrypting itself, this is not in order to say to us: I am a cipher. It may still conceal from us, without the slightest hidden intention, the secret that it shelters in its readability. It moves, fascinates, and seduces us all the more. The ellipsis and the caesura of discretion are in it; there is nothing it can do about it. This pass is a passion before becoming a calculated risk, prior to any strategy, prior to any poetics of ciphering intended [*destinée*], as in Joyce, to keep the professors busy for generations. Even supposing that this exhausts Joyce's first or true desire, something I do not believe, nothing seems to me more foreign to Celan.

Multiplicity and migration of languages, certainly, and within language itself. Babel: named in "Hinausgekrönt," after the "Ghetto-Rose" and that phallic figure knotted in the heart of the poem (*phallisch gebündelt*), this is also its last word, both its address and its sending.

> Und es steigt eine Erde herauf, die unsre,
> diese.
> Und wir schicken
> keinen der Unsern hinunter
> zu dir,
> Babel.

And an earth rises up, ours,
this one.
And we'll send
none of our people down
to you,
Babel.

Address and sending of the poem, yes, but what seems to be
said to Babel, addressed to it, is that nothing will be addressed to it.
One will send it nothing, nothing from us, none of ours.

Multiplicity and migration of languages, certainly, and
within language. Your country, it says, migrates all over, like
language. The country itself migrates and transports its borders.
It is displaced like the names and the stones that one gives as a
pledge, from hand to hand, and the hand is given, too, and what gets
carved out, cut off, torn away, can gather itself together anew in the
symbol, the pledge, the promise, the alliance, the partaken word, the
migration of the partaken word.

—was abriß, wächst wieder zusammen—
da hast du sie, da nimm sie dir, da hast du alle beide,
den Namen, den Namen, die Hand, die Hand,
da nimm sie dir zum Unterpfand,
er nimmnt auch das, und du hast
wieder, was dein ist, was sem war,

Windmühlen

stoßen dir Luft in die Lunge.
—what was cut off grows together again—
there you have it, so take it, there you have them both,

the name, the name, the hand, the hand,
so take them, keep them as a pledge,
he takes it too, and you have
again what is yours, what was his,

windmills

push air into your lungs.

Chance and risk of the windmill—language, which is related
as much to wind and mirage as it is to breath and spirit, to the
breathing bestowed. We will not recall all the ciphered trails of this
immense poem ("Es ist alles anders"), from Russia—"the name of
Osip"—to Moravia, to the Prague cemetery ("the pebble from /
the Moravian hollow / which your thought carried to Prague, / on to the
graves, to the grave, into life") and "near Normandy-Niemen," this
French squadron in war exile in Moscow, and so forth. Only this,
which speaks of the emigration of the country itself, and of its name.
Like language:

wie heißt es, dein Land
hinterm Berg, hinterm Jahr?
Ich weiß, wie es_heißt.
[...]
es wandert überall, wie die Sprache,
wirf sie weg, wirf sie weg,
dann hast du sie wieder, wie ihn,
den Kieselstein aus
der Mährischen Senke,
den dein Gedanke nach Prag trug.

what is it called, your country
behind the mountain, behind the year?
I know what it's called.
[...]
it wanders off everywhere, like language,
throw it away, throw it away,
then you'll have it again, like that other thing.
the pebble from
the Moravian hollow
which your thought carried to Prague.

Multiplicity and migration of languages, certainly, and
within language itself, Babel within a *single* language. *Shibboleth*
marks the multiplicity within language, insignificant difference as
the condition of meaning. But by the same token, the insignificance
of language, of the properly linguistic body: it can take on meaning
only in relation to a *place*. By place, I mean just as much the relation
to a border, country, house, or threshold as any site, any *situation*
in general from within which, practically, pragmatically, alliances
are formed, contracts, codes, and conventions established that give
meaning to the insignificant, institute passwords, bend language
to what exceeds it, make of it a moment of gesture and of step,
secondarize or "reject" it in order to find it again.

Multiplicity within language, or rather heterogeneity.
One should specify that untranslatability does not stem only from
the difficult passage (*no pasarán*), from the aporia or impasse
that isolates one poetic language from another. Babel is also this
impossible impasse, this *impossible pass* [*ce* pass impossible]—and
without transaction to come—stemming from the multiplicity of
languages within the uniqueness of the poetic inscription: several
times at once, several languages within a single poetic act. The

uniqueness of the poem, in other words, yet another date and *shibboleth*, forges and seals, in a single idiom, *in eins*, the poetic event, a multiplicity of languages and of equally singular dates. "In eins": within the unity and the uniqueness of this poem, the four languages are certainly not untranslatable, neither among themselves nor into other languages. But what will always remain untranslatable into any *other* language whatsoever is the marked difference of languages in the poem. We spoke of the *doing* that does not reduce to *knowing*, and of the *being able to do the difference* that comes down to *marking*. This is what goes on and what comes about here. Everything seems, in principle, *de jure,* translatable, except for the mark of the difference among the languages within the same poetic event. Let us consider, for example, the excellent French translation of "In eins." The German is translated into French, there's nothing more normal than that. *Schibboleth* and *no pasarán* are left untranslated, which respects the foreignness of these words in the principal medium, the German idiom of what one calls the original version. But in keeping, and how could one do otherwise, the French of this version in the translation, "Avec toi, / Peuple / de Paris," the translation must efface the very thing it keeps, the foreign effect of the French (unitalicized) in the poem, which places it in configuration with all the ciphers, passwords, and *shibboleths* that date and sign the poem, "In eins," in the unity—at once dissociated, torn, and adjoined, rejoined, regathered—of its singularities. There is no remedy to which translation could have recourse here, none, at least, in the body of the poem. No one is to blame; moreover, there is nothing to bring before the bar of translation. The *shibboleth*, here again, does not resist translation by reason of some inaccessibility of its meaning to transference, by reason of some semantic secret, but by virtue of that in it which forms the cut of a non-signifying difference in the body of the mark—written or oral, written in speech as a mark can be within a mark, an incision marking the very mark itself. On both sides of the historical, political, and linguistic border (a border is never natural), the meaning, the different meanings of the word *shibboleth* are known: river, ear of grain, olive twig. One even knows how it should be pronounced. But a single trial determines that some cannot while others can pronounce it with the heart's mouth. The first will not pass, the others will pass the line—of the place, of the country, of the community, of what takes place in a language, in languages as poems. Every poem has its own language; it is one time alone its own language, even and especially if several languages *are able* to cross there. From this *point of view*, which may become a watchtower, the vigilance of a sentinel, one sees well: the value of the *shibboleth* may always, and tragically, be inverted. Tragically because the inversion sometimes overtakes the initiative of subjects, the goodwill of men, their mastery of language and politics. Watchword or password in the struggle against oppression, exclusion, fascism, and racism, it may also corrupt its differential value, which is the condition of alliance and of the poem, making of it a discriminatory limit, the grillwork of policing, of normalization, and of methodical subjugation.

translated from the French by Joshua Wilner and Thomas Dutoit

CAST – AN UNSPOKEN PLAY
BASED ON TWO POEMS BY PAUL CELAN

Sawako Nakayasu

BEHIND: Initially curtain, scrim, mist, wall – of water, earth, sound.

CELLO: Invisible entry. True point of entry subject to perception, as sound crests above ocean-roar, volcano, envelope, wall.

WORDS: Accretion into an unstable mound. Volcanic. Threatened by ocean, by envelope.

PAIN: Shifts into ocean when advancing. Receding, returns to wall.
Surging mob floods over and above. Anti-creatures.

POWERS: Degrees. Counter to heaven.
Roar of anti-creatures and indecipherable things.

ANTI-
CREATURES: In front of arrival, hoist more flags.

TIME: Driving, driven. Runway.
Dissipated via flag carried atop arms of Words, Cello, Mob.

FLAG: Image flutters away from itself.
A copy is left behind.

REPLICA: Likewise.
                Towards time, ongoing, vainly.

YOU: Hurl forth another word-moon. Into space.

EVENING: Ebbs. Is climbed. Miracle.
                Thick with lungscrub.

WORD-MOON: Moonlight hits mound, reflects outward.
                Collects atop wordpile, invisibly, audibly.

LUNGSCRUB: Grows moss-like. Capillaries.

SMOKE-
CLOUDS: Two. Of breath, timber, cello.
                Sink into the book opened by the din of the
                temple.

SOMETHING: Grows true.
                Twelve times.
                Testifies.
                As a heart-shaped crater.
                Exposed.

BEYOND: Hit by arrows.
                Burned to the twelfth degree.

BLACK-
BLOODED
WOMAN: Drinks the black-blooded man's semen.

KING: Birth. Origins.
                Bare, beginnings.

ALL THINGS: Contraction, expansion.

—*Forward translation, transposition, and juxtaposition, via English and Japanese versions of "Wortaufschüttung" and "Cello-Einsatz"*

PAUL CELAN

Cid Corman

• *What in Celan's poetry makes it stand out from the mass of poetry currently produced?*

First of all—it wasn't *produced*; it was elicited. Elicited by a life which was drawn into the vortex of Holocaust—from which there was to be no escape—but only a deepening loss. The poetry is more than vent (from the pyramidal memory)—it is a revenge—a movement towards "justice"—playing the avenging angel. Hebraic in that.

Others have remarked the surrealistic fragmentation (which goes well beyond Goll)—the spitting-out of the beloved and hated language. *Odi et amo.* The self-hatred—the eroding—corrosive— undeniable and undenied—guilt. To HAVE survived. To have been born for this!

He has tasted the ash of language. And used it to write on the forehead of Hölderlin and Rilke and Trakl and Heidegger and Benn and others in other tongues. An unrelenting poetry—a suicidal poetry.

A poetry OF language—but of language AS livingdying— inextricably meaning parsed into meaninglessness. A tale told by an idiot.

It has an inexorable logic about it. A poetry that seems—now that we have it—had to be. A six-pointed star etched into our minds—a splintered star.

How could it not "stand out"?

• *What was your own response to Celan's work and has it affected your practice?*

In 1955—as I have written elsewhere (*SULFUR 2*)—I
met Celan through a mutually dear friend (Edith Aron). She
helped me make the first translations of his work into English
(perhaps into any other language). The first poem we did was—of
course—the DEATH FUGUE. I ended up translating ALL his
books as they appeared—until the posthumous work. The first two
books—apart from the obvious intensity and ring of the work—
didn't excite me *particularly*—beyond a handful of poems. But
from *SPRACHGITTER* (*Speechlattice*, 1959) I WAS impressed
profoundly. It was a direction I myself was moving in—the
probing of every word—every syllable—every pause and silence—
questioning meaning and trying to discover it IN THE EVENT. He
didn't alter my practice—he helped confirm it.

For me the Holocaust is human existence—trying to livedie
poetry at a time when most regard it as either indolence—evasion—
or at best amusement. Self-indulgence. Celan's "work" undermines
such regarding.

•*How does Celan's poetry relate to earlier and contemporary
movements in 20th Century poetry and art?*

Only as the Holocaust does: as the cry of a child in a room full
of dying people as the cyanide reaches them and they realize they are
immediately doomed by a cruelty that is both human and so the more
inhuman. A cry whose "value" is only the valor of cry. To reduce it
to some literary or art movement is to belittle what is little enough
anyhow—but all.

179

"SOUND SCRAPS, VISION SCRAPS":
PAUL CELAN'S POETIC PRACTICE

Marjorie Perloff

Thirty-four years after his death, Paul Celan's status as the
greatest German-language poet of the second half of the
twentieth century seems assured. His oeuvre—roughly 900
pages of poetry distributed over eleven volumes, 250 pages
of prose, more than 1,000 published correspondence, and
nearly 700 pages of poetry translated from eight languages—
has by now received massive critical attention....And yet the
work continues to be to a great extent terra incognita...

—Pierre Joris (2005)[1]

Paul Celan's reception, at least in the English-speaking world,
has always been connected to his status as great Holocaust Poet,
the poet who showed that, Adorno's caveat notwithstanding, it was
possible to write poetry, even great poetry, in the German language,
after Auschwitz. As "Poet, Survivor, Jew" (the subtitle of John
Felstiner's groundbreaking study of 1995),[2] Celan has become an
iconic figure: continental philosophers from Hans-Georg Gadamer to
Phillipe Lacoue-Labarthe have read Celan's poetic oeuvre as a post-
World War II Book of Wisdom. The result, ironically, has been to
place Celan in a kind of solitary confinement, a private cell where his
every "circumcised word" (Jacques Derrida's term)[3] can be examined

---

1   Pierre Joris, "Introduction," Paul Celan, *Selections*, ed. Pierre Joris (Berkeley:
University of California Press, 2005), p. 3.

2   John Felstiner, *Paul Celan: Poet, Survivor, Jew* (New Haven: Yale University
Press, 1995).

3   Jacques Derrida, "Shibboleth for Paul Celan," trans. Joshua Wilner, in Aris
Fioretos (ed.), *Word Traces: Readings of Paul Celan* (Baltimore: Johns Hopkins

for its allegorical weight and theological import, even as, so Pierre Joris suggests in the excellent introduction to his new *Selections*, its actual poetic forms and choices are largely ignored. "Perhaps the greatest risk for the reading of Celan in our time," writes the poet Charles Bernstein, "is that we have venerated him, in the process of removing him not only from his own time and place, but also from our own poetic horizon....[A] crippling exceptionalism has made his work a symbol of his fate rather than an active matrix for an ongoing poetic practice."[4]

It is that ongoing poetic practice I want to consider here. What follows is thus an experiment in reading Celan, not as exemplary Holocaust poet or as philosophical thinker, but quite simply as a mid-twentieth century poet. What, to begin with is Celan's radius of discourse? Is he a Modernist? A postmodernist? Does he believe that language can *signify* a reality outside itself? What is Celan's relationship to the various poetic currents dominant when he came of age? Is his a self-contained semiosis in the vein of John Ashbery? Or is Celan perhaps a proto-language poet? However unique a poet we take him to be, Celan does, after all, write out of a tradition, a culture, a history.

Suppose we take a poem often cited as conveying Celan's basic sense that the *ground* of language has become an *abyss*, that language is forced to speak the unspeakable. I am thinking of the title poem of *Sprachgitter* (1959), a title whose translation can only be reductive: *sprach* (past tense of *sprechen*) means "spoke," *Sprache* refers to both individual speech and language: in other words, to both *langue* and *parole*. As for *Gitter*, the noun designates "grate," "gate,"

University, 1994), pp. 3-72.

4   Charles Bernstein, "Celan's Folds and Veils," *Textual Practice* 18: 2 (Summer 2004): 200-01.

"fence," and "mesh" as well as "grille." "For fishermen," Anne Carson points out in her study of Celan and Simonides,[5] "it means a net or trap. For mineralogists, the lattice formation of a crystal." Whether fence or net, *Gitter* is always associated with some sense of blockage or obstruction. Here is the poem:

Sprachgitter

Augenrund zwischen den Stäben.

Flimmertier Lid
rudert nach oben,
gibt einen Blick frei.

Iris, Schwimmerin, traumlos und trüb:
der Himmel, herzgrau, muß nah sein.

Schräg, in der eisernen Tülle,
Der blakende Span.
Am Lichtsinn
errätst du die Seele.

(Wär ich wie du. Wärst du wie ich.
Standen wir nicht
unter einem Passat?
Wir sind Fremde.)

Die Fliesen. Darauf,
dicht beieinander, die beiden

---

5   Anne Carson, *Economy of the Unlost* (*Reading Simonides of Kios with Paul Celan)*, (Princeton: Princeton University Press, 1999), p. 30.

herzgrauen Lachen:
zwei
Mundvoll Schweigen.

Speech Grille

Eyeround between the bars.

Flitterbug lid
rows upward
sets a glance free.

Iris, swimmer, dreamless and dim;
the sky, heartgray, must be near.

Slanting, in the iron spout
the smouldering splinter.
By its lightsense
you guess the soul.

(Were I like you. Were you like me.
Did we not stand
under *one* Passat?
We are strangers.)

The flagstones. On them,
right next to each other, the two
heartgray puddles:
two

mouthfuls of silence. [my translation] [6]

---

6   Paul Celan, *Die Gedichte, Kommentierte Gesamtausgabe*, ed. with commentary by Barbara Wiedemann (Frankfurt: Suhrkamp, 2005), pp. 99-100. All further references to the German text are to this edition. Compare to the following three published translations:

    (1)   Joachim Neugroschel, in Joris, *Paul Celan: Selections* (California, 2005), pp. 63-64:

Speech-Grille
Eye-orb between the bars.

Ciliary lid
rows upwards,
releases a gaze.

Iris, swimmer, dreamless and dim:
the sky, heart-gray, must be near.

Skew, in the iron socket,
the smoldering splinter.
By the sense of light
you guess the soul.

(Were I like you. Were you like me.
did we not stand
under *one* tradewind?
We are strangers.)
The tiles. Upon them,
close together, the two
heart-gray pools:
two
mouthfuls of silence.

(2) John Felstiner, translator, *Selected Poems and Prose of Paul Celan* (New York: Norton, 2000), p. 107:

Speech-Grille

Round eyed between the bars.

Flittering lid

paddles upward,
breaks a glance free.

Iris, the swimmer, dreamless and drab:
heaven, heartgray, must be near.

Aslant, in the iron socket
a smoldering chip.
By sense of light
you hit on the soul.

(Were I like you. Were you like me.
Did we not stand
Under *one* trade wind?
We are strangers.)

The flagstones. On them,
close by each other, both
heartgray puddles:
two mouthfuls of silence.

(3) Anne Carson, *Economy of the Unlost*, pp. 31-32:

Language Mesh

Eyeround between the bars,
glimmeranimal lid
rows upward,
sets a look free.

Iris, swimmer, dreamless and dismal:
the sky heartgrey, must be near.

Slanted, in the iron socket
the smoking splinter
By its lightsense
you guess the soul.

(Were I like you. Were you like me.
Stand we not

Poststructuralist theorists have consistently taken "Speech Grille" as representative of Celan's post-Holocaust estrangement from language, an estrangement that culminates in what this particular poem refers to in the inscrutable *zwei / Mundvoll Schweigen*. In Jacques Derrida's famous essay "Shibboleth for Paul Celan," "Speech Grille" is cited in a discussion of the poet's "witness[ing] to the universal by virtue of absolute singularity," the singularity of the *Shibboleth*, that "word used as a test for detecting foreigners, or persons from another district, by their pronunciation," more loosely, "a catchword or formula adopted by a party or sect, by which their adherents or followers may be discerned, or those not their followers may be excluded."[7] The original *Shibboleth*, as the OED notes and as Derrida reminds us, was the Hebrew word used by Jephthah in *Judges*, xii 4-6, as a test-word by which to distinguish the fleeing Ephraimites (who could not pronounce the *sh*) from his own men, the Gileadites.[8] *Shibboleth*, Derrida argues, thus "marks the multiplicity within language, insignificant difference as the condition of meaning" (31). And that mark of difference or trace,

---

> under *one* tradewind?
> We are strangers.)
>
> The pavingstones. On them,
> tight by each other, the two
> heartgrey pools:
> two
> mouthfuls of silence

I have taken the liberty of retranslating the poem because all of the above have some rationalizations or slightly misleading renditions. Neugroschl's "orb of light" (line 1), for example, seems an overtranslation of "eyeround." Again, Carson's "dismal" for *trüb*" is too emphatic in the context. And the verb in line 12 must be in the past tense, as in the original. And so on.

7   See *Oxford English Dictionary* (161), Vol. 9, #2; Derrida, 55.

8   See OED, 1; Derrida 24-25.

which becomes comprehensible only in relation to a particular site or place," is, for Derrida, the key to Celan's poetic language. His is a "ciphered singularity: irreducible to any concept, to any knowledge," a "singularity which gathers a multiplicity *in eins*, and through whose grid a poem remains readable....The poem speaks, even should none of its references be intelligible, none other than the Other, the one to whom it addresses itself....Even if it does not reach and leave its mark on, at least it calls to, the Other. Address takes place" (35-36).

The Shibboleth must also be understood as a "circumcised word." The poet witnesses the universal—the wounding emblematized by circumcision, the Holocaust, death in general—"by virtue of absolute singularity, by virtue of and in the name of the other, the stranger, you toward whom I must take a step which, without bringing me nearer to you, without exchanging myself with you, without being assured passages, lets the word pass and assigns us, if not to the one, at least to the same. We were already assigned to it, dwelling beneath the same contrary wind" (35). The reference is to the fourth stanza of "Sprachgitter," with its reference to the strong Atlantic wind called Passat:

> (Were I like you. Were you like me.
> Did we not stand
>   under *one* Passat?
> We are strangers.)
>   (Derrida 55)

Strangers because we cannot speak the Shibboleth, the lost word (Holocaust, Jew, the exterminated family, death). The stanza above is thus one more instance of the inability of language to render the unspeakable, except as trace structure. *Circumcision,* Derrida posits, "designate[s] an operation, the surgical act of cutting, but also and equally the state, the quality, the condition of being circumcised" (63). The poetic word is opened only to be closed again; it names only to withdraw the name as soon as it is given. "The circumcised word is *first of all* written, at once both incised and excised in a body, which may be the body of a language and which in any case always binds the body to language" (67). More specifically it is also the German language that must be "circumcised," given that it had been debased by its status as the language of the Nazis (67). In Celan's own frequently cited words:

No matter how alive its traditions, with most sinister events in its Memory, most questionable developments around it, [German poetry] can no longer speak the language which many willing ears seem to expect. Its language has become more sober, more factual. It distrusts 'beauty'. It tries to be truthful. If I may search for a visual analogy while keeping in mind the polychrome of apparent actuality: it is a 'greyer' language, a language which wants to locate even its 'musicality' in such a way that it has nothing in common with the 'euphony' which more or less blithely continued to sound alongside the greatest horrors.[9]

In its "circumcised" version of the German language, Derrida suggests, Celan's poetry becomes an offering of something that the reader can never fully understand, a cipher of a language that can never quite speak the unspeakable and is hence a speaking silence. As Dennis J. Schmidt puts it, Celan's "'Two mouthfuls of silence' (*zwei / Mundvoll Schweigen*)...mark the place of the poem

---

9   Paul Celan, "Reply to a Questionnaire from the Flinker Bookstore, Paris, 1958," in *Collected Prose*, trans. Rosmarie Waldrop (New York: Sheep Meadow Press, 1986), pp. 15-16.

for Celan...such silence is not to be confused with mere quiet but needs to be heard as the unvocalized voice of the poem....a voice estranged from language, rendering the effort to listen to language in the poem rare, demanding, and painful at once."[10] And the classicist poet-philosopher Anne Carson reads *Sprachgitter* (in her translation, "Language Mesh") as "a word Celan uses to describe the operations of his own poetic language, in a poem about strangeness and strangers." And she asks:

> Does Celan use *Gitter* to imply passage, blockage or salvaging of speech? Mesh may do all these. Celan may mean all of these....The German language offers Celan a qualified hospitality, a murderously impure meal....Celan can make himself at home in his mother tongue only by a process of severe and parsimonious redaction....Mesh limits what he can say but may also cleanse it. As crystal it cleanses to the essence. As net it salvages what is cleansed. (Carson 30-31)

The "action of estrangement [that] takes place in this poem," Carson concludes, "represents, in some part, the condition of intimate alienation that obtained between Celan and his own language" (33).

The alienation of the poet from his own language, the status of a given word in that language as Shibboleth, designed to be misunderstood even by the Other addressed, the "mouthfuls of silence" the poet proffers the reader—these analyses of Celan's poetic are based, we should note, on a very particular set of assumptions about the way Celan's poetry—or, for that matter, any poetry—works. For Derrida in particular, a given poem is no more than an entrance into a larger poetic universe where particular

---

10   Dennis J. Schmidt, "Black Milk and Blue: Celan and Heidegger on Pain and Language," in *Hamacher* 110-29; see p. 110.

thematic motifs can be traced. Indeed, the book jacket copy for *Sovereignties in Question: The Poetics of Paul Celan,* the recently published book from Fordham University Press (2005) that brings together the 1984 "Shibboleth" with a number of later Derrida essays and interviews concerning Celan, contains the following description:

> Central themes include the date or signature and its singularity; the notion of the trace; temporal structures of futurity and the "to come"; the multiplicity of language and questions of translation; such speech acts as witness, promise, and testimony, but also lying and perjury; the possibility of the impossible; and, above all, the question of the poem as addressed and destined beyond knowledge, seeking to speak to and for the irreducible other....Derrida's approach to a poem is a revelation on many levels, from the most concrete ways of reading—for example, his analysis of a sequence of personal pronouns—to the most sweeping imperatives of human existence.

It is true that Derrida's "Shibboleth" contains some discussion of personal pronouns, of dates and place names, and of particular events commemorated in the poems, even as no single poem is discussed as a whole. From start to finish, Derrida mines the poems, short as most of them are, for particular lines or even single words that point to his larger interpretation of Celan's oeuvre. The "circumcised word," it seems, is one that is regularly taken out of context and linked to other related words so as to produce a coherent account of Celan's poetics. Moreover, in this discussion of lyric poetry—and here Derrida is representative of philosophical critics in general—nothing is said about sound structure, rhythm, lineation, syntax, or the actual organization of the poem in question.

190

Such reading, we might say, is more properly a reading *for*. Having found the phrase, *Nach /dem Unwiederholbaren* ("After / the unrepeatable") in *A La Pointe Acérée* (*Gedichte* 146), the strategy is to find echoes and analogues of *Das Unwiederholbare* and its relationship to the *Herzgewordenes* ("what has become heart"), never mind the surrounding details.

As such, the name Celan has become a cipher for profundity, for the true voice of the Holocaust in all its horror and pain—a voice that of necessity presents what Werner Hamacher has called "a language which appears at odds with itself" (Hamacher xi). Celan, writes Anne Carson, "is a poet who uses language *as if he were always translating*" (28). Pierre Joris similarly remarks that "Celan's language, though German on the surface, is a foreign language, even for native speakers....The Celanian dynamic...involves a complex double movement...of love for his mother tongue and of...strife against her murderers who are the originators and carriers of that same tongue."[11] This emphasis on double movement is even more prominent in Adorno: "Celan's poems," he notes, "want to speak of the most extreme horror through silence. Their truth content itself becomes negative. They imitate a language beneath the helpless language of human beings, indeed beneath all organic language: It is that of the dead speaking of stones and stars."[12]

A language beyond all organic language, a language that looks like translation rather than "original," a language at odds with itself, Shibboleth, circumcised word, and so on. How do we reconcile such views with Celan's own insistence that "This language, notwithstanding its inalienable complexity of expression, is

---

11   Pierre Joris. "Introduction," Paul Celan, *Breathturn*, trans. Pierre Joris (Los Angeles: Sun & Moon, 1995), p. 42.

12   Theodor Adorno. *Aesthetic Theory*, p. 322.

191

concerned with *precision*. It does not transfigure or render 'poetical'; it names, it posits, it tries to measure the area of the given and the possible"? (*Collected Prose* 16). In what follows, I want to explore that "precision"—what Ezra Pound called the "luminous detail"—by reading Celan, not as the "special case" he is usually taken to be, but as a sophisticated postwar European poet, whose native language and culture were German—more specifically the German of the Austro-Hungarian Empire into which he was born—but whose mature years were lived in France, with his wife Gisèle de Lestrange, a woman from an aristocratic, Catholic background, and his son Eric. His real last name *Antschel* had become, by a kind of anagram, the French-sounding Celan.

2. **On the Fence**

In a draft for "The Meridian" (the speech Celan gave on the occasion of receiving the Georg Büchner Prize in 1960), the poet notes, "The pictorial" (*Bildhaftes*), that is by no means something visual; it is, like everything connected to speech, a mental phenomenon...a manifestation of speech as something derived from writing, therefore from something that is silent." And he adds the parenthetical note (*Sprachgitter, das ist auch das* Sprechgitter, *macht das sichtbar* ["Speech-grille, that is also speak-grille, makes that evident]" (*Gedichte 643*). The German word *Sprechgitter* is not a neologism. On the contrary, it refers to an object to be found at hardware or electric stores: namely, the transom above or below the doorbell, used in apartment or office buildings to announce one's arrival and desire to be buzzed in [figure 1]. As such, a *Sprechgitter* serves as the conduit from a speaker's voice to that of an unseen (and perhaps unknown) addressee—a situation that, as we shall see, is indeed germane to Celan's poem.

But *Sprechgitter* is also an architectural term, relating to the medieval church. In the notes to the Suhrkamp *Gesamtausgabe* (*Gedichte* 652-53) Barbara Wiedemann informs us that *Sprachgitter* was written in response to a picture postcard Celan received from the author and publisher Günther Neske, with whom he planned to publish his next collection.[13] The card, dated *Pfingsten* (Whitsuntide) 1957, bears the image of the fourteenth-century *Sprechgitter* or Confessional Screen [figure 2] of the former convent church (1300) called *Klarissenkloster* at Pfullingen in Württemberg, [figure 3]. The *Sprechgitter* pictured on the card was, according to the official guide to the Visit of German Monuments, "the only contact the convent's nuns had with the outside world."[14]

The *Klarissenkloster* itself was named for Santa Clara of Assisi (1194-1253). According to legend, the aristocratic eighteen-year old Clara, having fallen under the spell of St. Francis's preaching [see figure 4], secretly left her father's house in the dark of night, and "proceeded to the humble chapel of the Porziuncula, where St. Francis and his disciples met her with lights in their hands. Clara then laid aside her rich dress, and St Francis, having cut off her hair, clothed her in a rough tunic and a thick veil, and in this way the young heroine vowed herself to the service of Jesus Christ."[15] From then on, no one in the outside world saw Clara again. As foundress of the Order of Poor Ladies, also known as Poor Claras, she lived in the strictest poverty. In her later years as Abbess, Clara helped the blind and ill St. Francis by erecting a little wattle hut for him in an olive grove close to the monastery; it was here that he composed

---

13   *Gedichte* 632. In the event, the volume was published by S. Fischer instead.

14   See <http: tag-des-offenen-denmals.de/laender/bw/reis_reutlingent/ pfullingen>.

15   See entry on "St. Clare of Assisi," *Catholic Encyclopedia*, <http:www. newadvent.org/cathen/04004a.htm>.

his famous "Canticle of the Sun." Another time, Clara defended her convent from the troops of Frederick II, who were trying to enter by a ladder placed against an open window of the abbey. She raised the ciborium bearing the Host so high that the soldiers fell backward as if dazzled, and the others who were ready to follow them took flight. Both these stories—the transfiguration of the blind St. Francis and the dazzling of the invading army of Frederick II—fostered the belief that the Holy Water of the Church of Santa Clara in Assisi could cure those with eye-diseases, and it was hence referred to, in a nice pun, as *aqua clara*. The abbess was canonized in 1255. In 1958, a year before the publication of Celan's *Sprachgitter*, Pope Pius XII also declared Santa Clara to be the patroness of *television* because of her legendary ability to see into the distance.[16]

Celan's poem, prompted by Neske's picture postcard, contains a network of references to the eye and its inability to see. The opening line, *Augenrund zwischen den Stäben* ("Eyeround between the bars"), presents the image of the poet's eye (or is it the priest's behind the confessional screen?) trying to penetrate the bars so as to *see* what is on the other side. The coinage *Augenrund* can also refer to the round made by the poet's eyes making a circle as they take in the scene and try to penetrate what is *behind* or inside the *Stäben*. The theme is carried on in the next two stanzas: the "shimmering" eyelid "rows" upward, stealing a glance at the ceiling. And beneath that lid, "swims" the iris, dreamless and dim or drab. A "swimming" iris means a watery or blurred eye; indeed, it can be the sign of the detachment of the retina.

In Greek mythology, Iris is the Goddess of the Rainbow, the swift-footed messenger of the Gods, who often assumed the shape of a mortal, known only to those who received her message. When

---

16   See the Catholic Encyclopedia online: http://www.newadvent.org/cathen/

a quarrel arose among the gods, Zeus sent Iris to the river Styx in the Underworld to bring back the golden jug of sacred water, which signified the oath of the gods. But in "Speech-Grille," the blurry iris beneath the flickering lid suggests that the message of the Gods, like the healing *aqua clara* of the Abbey, cannot penetrate the speech screen. There is no response from its other side. Hence the poet posits that a "heartgray" sky, its gloom reflected in the dark, dim iris, must be near—a sky in which the rainbow of the Covenant is nowhere to be glimpsed.

The fourth stanza introduces a new image, but one which metonymically relates to the eye. *Schräg in der eisenern Tülle, / der blakende Span*: *Tülle*, meaning spout, also brings to mind the silken fabric called Tüll (*tulle* in French); *Span* is a shaving or splinter. What is this smoldering splinter, slanting in its silken or silvery container? If we assume that the speaker facing the grille, a speaker whose eyelid "rows" upward to take a glance at what is above, has entered a church, the iron spout, seen at an angle, is probably a censer, hanging from the ceiling [figure 5]. The roundness of the censer matches the "eyeround" of line 1, even as the smoking splinter within it is analogous to a mote in the poet's eye—the mote that evidently makes the iris swim, the dream fade, and the lid shimmer or flicker. The conclusion drawn in lines 9-10 thus seems nothing if not logical: it is the "lightsense" experienced by the churchgoer that animates the soul, the "lightsense" Clara could offer to the blind St. Francis and the invaders at the abbey's gate. But here there is no light: the soul remains in darkness.

What the poet is suggesting is that for him, there is no grace of God, not only not in this Christian church, but perhaps nowhere. His companion, however, mentioned for the first time in line 11 (and most probably a veiled allusion to Celan's French Catholic wife Gisèle de Lestrange) may be reacting differently. Hence the question:

195

Were I like you. Were you like me.
Did we not stand
Under *one* Passat?

These lines (placed in parentheses, of which more below) express
the poet's painful desire to be *at one* with his wife, to *share* with her
as his other. But the recognition (line 14) is that this is not the case:
"We are strangers." Hence, on leaving the church, the flagstones are
always and only flagstones, and these, in turn, are covered by two
"heartgray" *Lachen* (note the repetition of the adjective used in line
6). *Lachen*, in this context, has the primary meaning of puddles or
pools: two gray pools of water blot the flagstones. But *Lachen* also
means "notches"—the stones are notched with the sign of the two
unknown strangers—and in the singular, the noun "Lachen" is the
common word "laughter"—in this case, a mirthless, hollow chuckle
of sorts. In all three cases, the flagstones reflect the "heartgray"
condition of the lovers: the desire for communion—with hidden
priest? God? and especially the "you" who is his beloved—has
failed. All that remains are their two mouthfuls of silence. The
poem's conclusion links sight and speech: both are, at least for the
moment, suspended. As Celan wrote his friend Joachim Seng, "I
tell myself that in *Sprachgitter* the existential, the difficulty of all
speaking (to one another) and at the same time the structure of that
speaking is what counts" (*Gedichte* 643).

To say, as does Hamacher, that a poem like "Speech-Grille"
embodies a "language at odds with itself," or that, in Anne Carson's
words, *Sprachgitter* represents "the condition of intimate alienation
that obtained between Celan and his own language," may well be
true as a generality, but it doesn't get us very far. For here—and this
is usually the case in Celan's work—the issues are quite specific.

To be literal: the poet and his wife have evidently wandered into an unnamed abbey church; the poet eyes the confessional screen or barred side chapel, ruminating on whether he can, in Wordsworth's words, "see into the life of things," if he can see make contact with God or at least with his companion. But there is a mote in his eye, figured by the splinter in the swinging censer, as by the tick in his eyelid and the "swimming" of his iris; this poet is neither a reliable messenger nor does a message from outside come through to him. It is not so much speech but vision that fails and the heart that shuts. Does his companion feel the same way? Evidently not, so that separation occurs: the watery eyes of the suppliants are replaced by two gray puddles, or again, the mote in the poet's eye becomes the "heartgray" notch on the stone. Blockage prevents both vision and speech.

   Sprachgitter can thus be read, first and foremost, as a poem about failed love, failed communion, both between lovers and between the poet and his God. As in the case of Santa Clara, the outside world—what Yeats called the "emperor's drunken soldiery"—recedes. And that failure of communication, critics like Joris and Carson have noted, spells out a necessary alienation not only from the poet's *intimates* and friends but from the German language itself. In 'Memory of Words" (1990), the poet Edmund Jabès maintains that "the German language, though it is the one in which [Celan] immersed himself, is also the one which for a time those who claimed to be its protectors had forbidden him. If it is indeed the language of his pride, it is also that of his humiliation.... There is something paradoxical...to totally invest yourself in the language of a country that rejects you."[17] But, strictly speaking—and here I think we must be strict—Germany had never been Celan's

17   Edmond Jabès, *La mémoire des mots* (Paris: Fourbis, 1990); trans. Pierre Joris, in Joris, *Celan Selections*, 217-223; see p. 217.

country, and his language, as deformed and unsituated as it seems to be, should perhaps also be understood as the language of Karl Kraus and Robert Musil, rather than primarily that of the poet's "humiliation." True, "Speech-grille" contains a number of elaborate neologisms, beginning with the title—*Sprachgitter, Augenrund, Flimmertier*—and unusual compounds such as *herzgrau* and *Lichtsinn* as well as exotic references like "Passat" (the standard, but foreign-sounding German term for trade wind). But on the whole the syntactic locutions, if not the diction, seem familiar enough, especially to an Austrian ear like mine. And here we must remember that Celan's German was never that of Berlin or Frankfurt but the German of Vienna, which was the center and magnet of the Austro-Hungarian Empire, into which Celan was belatedly born in 1920, two years after its dissolution. For his parents, the "official" German of Vienna was the necessary language of the educated class: Paul's mother Fritzi always spoke German to her son and taught him the German classics. Such colloquial locutions as *gibt einen Blick frei, der Himmel muß nah sein, errätst du die Seele*, or *Wär ich wie du. Wärst du wich ich*, testify to the naturalness, if only an intermittent one, of Celan's speech-base. He was, in other words, more at home in German—his particular variant of German—than he or his readers were given to admit. Then, too, we must remember that Celan lived in Vienna from 1947 to '48 before moving to Paris—and that he had an intense affair—and drawn-out correspondence—with the Austrian writer Ingeborg Bachmann.

Indeed, the difficulty of Celan's lyric has less to do with word choice or even word order than with the absence of any and all connective tissue, whether causal, temporal, or even paratactic, in his poetic discourse. What is missing, for starters, are the pronouns. *Augenrund zwischen den Stäben*: we surmise that the eye is the poet's own but we cannot be sure, and lines 2-4 provide

198

no clues. In line 5, "Iris" is represented in the third person, as "The Swimmer" (female noun), and hence evokes the goddess as well as the poet's eye. The abrupt introduction of "du" in line 11 thus comes as something of a shock: here, suddenly and parenthetically, is an address to another person. But after the announcement that "We are strangers" in line 14, the poem lapses back into its blank, subjectless third-person mode, culminating in those mouthfuls (whose?) of silence.

In the same vein, a given line rarely prepares us for the next. It is not a foregone conclusion, for example, that because the iris is a swimmer, "dreamless and dim," that the sky must be equally drab and grey. Again, the perspective of the smoking splinter in lines 7-8 does not explain why or how the "Lightsense" allows us to guess the soul's status. And there are no signals to indicate the shift from indoors to outdoors between lines 14 and 15. This is, in other words, an extremely oblique lyric, stripped of temporal and spatial markers that might explain what is going on. Then, too, pun and allusion produce great density: "Iris" is both the colored part of the eye and the Greek Goddess, "tulle" suggests cloth as well as spout, "lightsense" can be the yearning for light (think of St. Francis) but also the unbearable lightness of being, which may define the soul. And the Passat wind looks and sounds like *Passah*, German for Pesach or Passover;[18] it thus interjects a Jewish note into the otherwise Christian imagery.

Other poets—Mallarmé in French, Hölderlin in German, Emily Dickinson in English—have written lyric as obscure and condensed as Celan's. Dickinson, for that matter, introduces at least as many neologisms as does Celan, and her syntax is equally complex and disjunctive. Like Dickinson, Celan uses extensive

---

18   See Felstiner, *Celan* 107.

sound patterning to relate what is otherwise disparate. Consider the internal rhyme of *Flimmertier—Schwimmerin—Himmel*, the alternate alliteration of *Dicht beieinander die beiden*, the alliteration of *traumlos und trüb*, of *Himmel, herzgrau*, and of *darauf, / dicht*. The dominant rhythm of line 1:

/　x　∧　　　/　x　　　x　/　x

Augenrund　zwischen　den Stäben

where a dactyl, whose third syllable has secondary stress, is followed by trochee and ambiphrach, is repeated in truncated form in line 2:

/　x　∧　　/

Flimmertier　Lid

And with variations throughout. The penultimate line with its \break after the monosyllabic *Zwei*, produce the final tongue twister:

/　∧　　　　/

Mundvoll　Schweigen

Here the heavy consonants sound as if the words are hard to spit out, as indeed they are. Sounds of silence would be one thing, but mouthfuls of being silent, of refusing or being unable to speak, have a sinister edge, drowning the poignancy of those eight monosyllables of the utmost simplicity—

/　x　x　/　‖　/　x　x　/

Wär ich wie du.　wärst du wie ich.

—a conditional that cannot be satisfied despite the rhythmic identity between the two hemistychs.

Finally, a word about punctuation. Celan's opening line, a suspended noun phrase, would seem to need no punctuation, yet Celan concludes it with a period, thus emphasizing its separation from what follows. Similarly "Wär ich wie du" ends, not on a note of question, as the intonation may suggest, but again with two periods, the punctuation itself implying that there is no match between the first conditional and the second. Indeed, the short non-sentences closed by periods retain their separate identity. More important, the whole fifth stanza is placed in parentheses, as if to suggest that the actual conversation between "I" and "you" occurs only in memory or perhaps in supposition; it stands outside the main frame, itself a kind of *Augenrund* ("eyeround") between the bars that separate the poet from his interlocutor. Confession, that is to say, cannot take place.

Such overpunctuation becomes a Celan signature, as in *Engführung* ("Stretto"), where we find passages like the following:

Asche.
Asche, Asche.
Nacht.
Nacht-und-Nacht.—Zum
Aug geh, zum feuchten.

        Zum

           Aug geh,
           Zum feuchten—
              (*Gedichte* 114-15)

Ashes.
Ashes, ashes.
Night.
Night-and-night.—To

the eye, go, to the moist.

To

the eye, go,
to the moist—[19]

Here the poetic tension arises from the simple repetition
that should be incantatory but is just the opposite because of the
passage's line-breaks and punctuation, creating a feverish rhythm.
I am reminded of such Wallace Stevens titles as "How to Live.
What to Do—" a title whose poignancy surely has a lot to do with
the period rather than expected comma after the word "Live." The
comma would supply continuity, the drive toward a way of being.
But the period suggests that the poet feels there is no way to live.
The sentence merely stops. Similar effects are found within Steven's
later poems: for example, in "No Possum, No Sop, No Taters," the
couplets are overpunctuated, as in:

> It is deep January. The sky is hard.
> The stalks are firmly rooted in ice.

And in "Debris of Life and Mind" the final couplet reads:

> The most gay and yet not so gay as it was.
> Stay here. Speak of familiar things a while.[20]

Late Modernist poetry—Celan's, Stevens's, or, for example,
Beckett's poetic prose, is characterized by such condensation and

---

19   Robert Kelly, trans. in Joris, Celan Selections, p. 69.

20   *The Collected Poems of Wallace Stevens* (New York: Alfred A. Knopf, 1961),
pp. 293, 338.

reduction of its symbolist base, its dissolution of the speaking subject into the fragmented world it inhabits. But it remains, I would argue, a "high" mode of lyric discourse, avoiding the popular culture references, verbal-visual disjunctions, shifts from comic to serious, and found text of the poetry to come in the later twentieth century.

Then, too, this is a poetry that still respects—as later poetry will not—the emblematic status of the natural and human world. Celan's imagery—eye, mouth, grass, stone, flower, tree—is the imagery of Dickinson and Stevens as well; but for Celan, the natural world always bears the imprint of technological invention as well. Consider the late minimalist poem in *Atemwende* ("Breathturn," 1965) that gave Celan's 1967 volume its title:

> FADENSONNEN
> Über der grauschwarzen Ödnis,
> Ein baum-
> Hoher Gedanke
> Greift sich den Lichtton: es sind
> Noch Lieder zu singen jenseits
> Der Menschen.   (*Gedichte 179*)

> THREADSUNS
> above the greyblack wastes.
> A tree-
> high thought
> grasps the light-tone: there are
> still songs to sing beyond
> mankind.[21]

---

21   *Gedichte* 179; Celan, *Breathturn*, trans. Pierre Joris (Los Angeles: Sun & Moon, 1995), p. 84.

Apollinaire's great 1913 poem, "Zone," concludes with the startling image of the setting sun as a cut-throat: *soleil cou coupé*. But for Apollinaire, the sun still existed, a perfect sphere, an orb of light, or ball of fire that might be perceived as cut off. For Celan, by contrast, there is no more single sun—no center, no point of origin—only a multiplicity of threadsuns—thin slivers of sun or light rays, fragile and breakable. The poet's life hangs, so to speak, by a sun-thread above the gray-black wasteland in which he dwells. But in line 3 a tree-high thought counters his despair, for it "grasps the light-tone." The English translation, which suggests that the German noun means no more than a "light tone" or "tone of light" is deceptive, for *Lichtton* is a technical term from the annals of early sound film. The *Welte* Light-Tone or Light-Organ, invented in Germany in 1936 [figure 6] was an electronic instrument using electro-optically controlled tone generators. As the Welte website informs us, "A glass disk was printed with 18 different waveforms giving three different timbres for all the octave registers of each single note. The glass tone wheel rotated over a series of photoelectric cells, filtering a light beam that controlled the sound timbre and pitch."[22]

If we thus think of "light-tone" as a controlled sound pitch mechanically produced on celluloid film, the poem's thrust becomes obvious. Like Stevens's "palm at the end of the mind," "stand[ing] on the edge of space," in "Of Mere Being,"[23] Celan's "tree-high thought" grasps for the sound pitch that allows his own particular film-strip to come to life. "There are," it seems, "still songs to sing beyond / mankind." A *Sprachgitter*, let us recall, is not an impenetrable language wall; its openings allow the threadsuns

---

22   See *Lichtton website:* http://www.obsolete.com/120_years/machines/light_tone_organ/

23   Wallace Stevens. "Of Mere Being." *The Palm at the End of the Mind: Selected Poems and a Play.* ed. Holly Stevens. (New York: Archon Books, 1984), p. 398.

of song to come through, even as "The wind moves slowly in the branches," of Stevens's palm. Indeed, to read Celan against the late Stevens is to become aware that, by midcentury, Pound's Imagist credo that "The natural object is always the adequate symbol," had given way to a curious sleight-of-hand whereby an image like *Lichtton* ("light-tone") can morph into an obscure—but highly specific—reference, in this case to the new technology of the period.

Such odd shifts are by no means unique to Celan: his contemporary Samuel Beckett, for example, was fond of introducing arcane words like *ravanastron* (an Indian stringed instrument played with a bow) into the texture of otherwise flat, sober descriptions by his protagonists, in this case, Watt. But just as Beckett's ravanastron hangs on an ordinary wall in a "large bare white room,"[24] so Celan's "threadsunned" *Lichtton* is found among the "heartgray" puddles on the paving stones. It is this tension between the Imagist-Symbolist model of the early century and the "illegible" texts to come that makes Celan's lyric poetry so challenging—a pivot in the tradition that takes us from Hölderlin, Dickinson, and Mallarmé to the elliptical fragments of Wallace Stevens, George Oppen, and Susan Howe. I conclude with the following seven-line poem from *Lichtzwang* (*Lightduress*):

> WAS ES AN STERNEN BEDARF
> schüttet sich aus,
>
> deiner Hände laubgrüner Schatten
> sammelt es ein,
>
> freudig zerbeiß ich

---

24   Samuel Beckett, *Watt* (1953; London: John Calder 1976), p. 68.

das münzenkernige
Schicksal.

WHAT'S REQUIRED OF STARS,
pours itself out.

your hands' leafgreen shadow
gathers it in.

joyfully I bite in two
coin-powered
fate.   (*Gedichte* 287, my translation)

Here syntax seems uncomplicated, the only obscure word being
münzenkernige. This compound combines *Münzen* ("coins") with the
adjective *kernig* for "robust," "strong," "powerful," the neologism
formed on the analogy of the epithet "high-powered." But, as in the
case of such related texts as Beckett's *Imagination Dead Imagine*
(which, incidentally, has often been said to refer to a crematorium),
we know what the words "say" well enough, but not what they
mean. "What's required of stars" is surely their light—a light that is
"gathered" or collected into the foliage-green or "leafgreen shadow"
of "your hands." But does such gathering dissipate the shadow or
vice-versa? And does biting one's coin-powered destiny in half mark
resignation to one's fate or the triumph above it? "You know," we
read in Stevens's "Of Mere Being," "that it is not the reason / That
makes up happy or unhappy." But the speech-grille remains open,
poised to receive those words that pour themselves into the waiting
shadows.

FIGURES

Figure 1

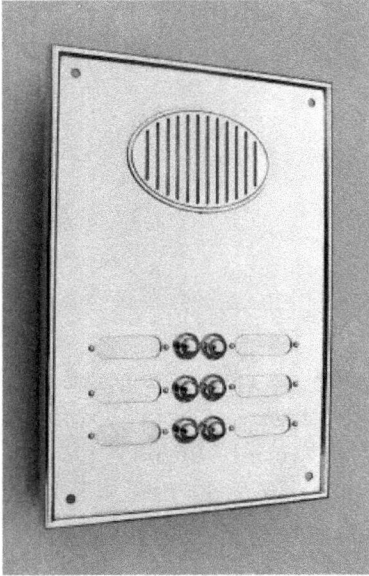

Figure 1. Klingelplatte "Milano" 200m x 300m—Firma Replicata, Deutschland, website www.replicta.de

Figure 2

Figure 2. Confessional Box, Church at Oradour, 14th C. http://www.
oradour.info/images/orconfes.htm/ Image of Pfullingen confessional
did not reproduce well but this is quite similar. French travel site.

Figure 3

Figure 3. Klosterkirche, Pfüllingen, Deutschland. C. 1300. Restored 1539. www.pfullingen.de/images/orte/klosterkirche.Jpg 432 x 435 pixels - 23k [Pfullingen, Wurtemberg Chamber of Commerce)

Figure 4

Figure 4. Santa Clara of Assisi as a little girl with St. Francis,
depicted in "Heiligen Klara von Assisi: Leben der Klara von Assisi:
http://santachiara.san-francesco.org/

Figure 5

Figure 5. Smoking censer in medieval church http://www.vam.ac.uk/
vastatic/microsites/bbchistory/Images/Censer/Censerlarge.jpg/

Figure 6

Figure 6. Welte *Licht-Ton* or *Light Organ,* 1936: http://www. obsolete.com/120_years/

(No permissions needed—1 and 6 are shops in Germany, 2 and 3 are travel sites, 4 is encyclopedia article, 5 is illustrative church article)

PAUL CELAN: A MEMOIR AND A POEM

Jerome Rothenberg

My sense, circa 1958, was that I was the first poet to
translate Celan into English.[1] We exchanged a sketchy letter or two,
but I didn't meet him until 1967, while I was traveling with my wife
and son in Europe. For me, Celan was clearly the great one among
those "new young German poets" I had translated, but his continuing
work seemed so intrinsically locked into its own language that I held
off from anything past *Mohn und Gedächtnis* and *Sprachgitter*. Still,
there had been some questions about taking it further, and when it
was again suggested by Alan Brilliant and Teo Savory of Unicorn
Books, I took it as a chance to be in contact with Celan again and
possibly to meet him.

I believe I made the arrangements from London, where we
were staying with Stuart and Deidre Montgomery. I really wanted to
meet Celan, and he seemed easy enough about it, so we made plans
that when I came to Paris, I would drop over one afternoon to the
École Normale, and we would spend some time together. My only
discomfort was that I wasn't serious about translating him at length,
while fearing that he probably only knew me as a translator.

My own poetry at that time was moving into the ancestral
work of *Poland/1931*—the very beginnings of that. But Celan,
although he was kind enough to acknowledge one of my earlier
books, would have had no way of knowing about "The Wedding"
or "The King of the Jews" or the "Satan in Goray" poem for Isaac
Bashevis Singer, which I had then written and had been performing
for the first time in London. For my own part, I wasn't yet aware of
the turn towards visionary and brilliant judaisms his work had taken

---

1   Jerome Rothenberg (ed.), *New Young German Poets* (City Lights Books,
1959). The poem, "a letter to Paul Celan in memory," is reprinted from Jerome
Rothenberg's *Vienna Blood* (New Directions, 1980) by permission of the author.

in *Die Niemandsrose* and so on. It is important to say that, because the Jewish thing was what we largely spoke about—with more ambivalence on both sides than I can summon up by way of concrete recollection.

I don't know what café we went to from the École, but we stayed there for two or three hours, drinking wine and speaking. He was—as I knew he would be—different in appearance from the American and British poets I knew, who in the now distant 1960s were glowing in the extravagance of new-found beards and shining flower shirts. Celan's whole manner was conservative, even (dare I say it?) drab. Dark and catlike, he spoke softly, nervously, in German and in broken English, as we tried to find a common language.

I kept no record of the conversation, which accordingly has been reduced to stories told over the intervening years. A part of the time we ran over the names of poets we knew in common—with Celan, I remember, very edgy about his German contemporaries and their too easy relation (I think the point was) to the language and the culture. We spoke about America and his desire to visit—not only to read his poetry here, but to visit an old relative who was then living in Chicago. He wasn't aware of much recognition in the States (just the opposite: he thought he had been snubbed here), and he was certainly suspicious of most poets who had approached him with proposals to translate his work.

But the burden of the conversation fell increasingly on the idea of "Jewishness"—his discovery of his own and his concern about his translators' ability to share or understand it. We exchanged some Jewish stories. He spoke about the war and the camps—and very glowingly about the poetry of Nelly Sachs. I told him I had been asked to do some versions of Yiddish poets, and he suggested that I try the work of Eliezer Steinberg. I mentioned meeting Singer, but my recollection is he drew a blank on that one.

214

The talk on both sides was punctuated by questions and clarifications—the need to speak more clearly or more slowly, since what we were doing was a combination of German and English (clear German, clear English, halting German, halting English). It is a common enough experience, but it stands out sharply from that day because at the end of it—as we were leaving the cafe—I thought to ask him if he spoke Yiddish. His reply was that while he had not been raised as a Yiddish speaker, he learned it during the war. I, on the other hand, had grown up in New York City, but I had spoken *only* Yiddish to the age of three or four. So, after all that stammering talk about Jewishness and language, we did in fact have a common (Jewish) language that we could speak, although we hadn't tried to speak it.

I never saw Celan after that, and I don't remember if we communicated further. The following year I dedicated the early poems of *Poland/1931* to him, and five years after his death, I wrote the following poem, which incorporates some of his own words, including the Yiddish one that ends it. Now as then, I find Celan's relation to language marvelous and shattering. I trust that the anecdotal tone of what I've written here doesn't in any way detract from that.

* * *

12/75
a letter to Paul Celan in memory

    of how your poems
    arise in me
    alive
    my eye fixed on

your line
"light was salvation"
I remember
(in simpler version)
Paris
nineteen sixty seven
in cold light of
our meeting
shivered to dumbness
you said "jew"
& I said "jew"
though neither spoke
the jew words
jew tongue
neither the mother language
loshen
the vestiges of holy speech
but you said
"pain"
under your eyebrows
I said "image"
we said "sound"
& turned around to
silence   lost
between two languages
we drank wine's words
like blood
but didn't drink toward
vision   still
we could not speak
without a scream

a guttural
the tree
out of the shadow of
the white cafe was not
"the tree"
roots of our speech
above us
in the sun
under the sewers
language of the moles
"who dig & dig
"do not grow wise
"who make no song
"no language
into the water silence
of your death
in the pink pale sky of Paris
in the afternoon
that held no constellations
no knowledge of the sun
as candelabrum
tree   menorah
"light knotted into air
"with table set
"chairs empty
"in sabbath splendor
the old man stood beside
in figure of a woman
raised his arms to reach
axis of the world
would bring the air down

solidly
and speak no sound
the way you forced
my meaning
to your poem
the words of which still press
into my tongue
"drunk
"blesst
"*gebentsht*

PAUL CELAN MEETS SAMUEL BECKETT

John Felstiner

He does not meet him.

Living alone in March 1970 (with never-healing wounds) on Avenue Émile Zola just across from Pont Mirabeau, apart from his wife Gisèle and son Eric, this "true-stammered mouth," survivor of "the thousand darknesses of deathbringing speech," has recently returned from a fortnight in Israel, his first visit, elated and drawn to move there but fearful of yet again losing his German mother tongue, his beloved mother's tongue seized as if overnight by her murderers. Franz Wurm, a poet-friend in Paris, invites him one afternoon to come along and meet Beckett, but Celan says No—to go unannounced at the last minute isn't right. That evening, given greetings from Beckett, he says: *That's probably the only man here I could have had an understanding with.*

But hadn't there already been an understanding, hadn't they been meeting all along, those years in Paris—the older man a more-or-less voluntary Irish exile to France and French, the younger man, orphaned, homelandless, reaching Paris but cleaving to German: Beckett chipping away at silence with "this dust of words," Celan with his "gasping words," with the "prayer-sharp knives / of my / silence"? During the 1953 opening run of *En attendant Godot*, where Didi and Gogo go on "blathering about nothing in particular," Celan composed "The Vintagers," in which "bent toward blindness and lamed," a "latemouth" thirsts for wine, a "crook-stick speaks into / the silence of answers."

Around that time, for his students at the École Normale Supérieure (where Beckett had taught English years earlier), Celan chose a passage from Beckett's novel *L'Innomable* (The Unnamable) to translate into German: "And yet I am afraid, afraid of what my words will do to me, to my refuge, yet again....If I could speak and yet say nothing, really nothing? Then I might escape being gnawed to death."

Among thousands of books in Celan's private library, many reveal sharp marginal notes, underscorings, sidescorings, dissents, exclamations. Yet the Beckett volumes show none of these. Why? Did the author of *Endgame* and *Krapp's Last Tape* and *Texts for Nothing* cut too close to the bone for Celan to take a detached stance?

In 1961, hearing that his German publisher might be meeting Beckett at the Closerie des Lilas, Celan too goes to the café—but nothing comes of it. The years drive on: Celan's charged poems join him with Beckett as Europe's only authentic writers "after Auschwitz," in Adorno's view. Meanwhile his malaise harshens terribly.

Man hat mich zerheilt, "They've healed me to pieces," Celan writes an Israeli friend about the doctors' "simplistic" attempts to fix a psychic "damage reaching to the core of my existence." His last weeks, in late winter and early spring of 1970, seesaw between despair and determination.

"I have come to you in Israel because I needed to," Celan tells a group of writers there. While he's in Jerusalem, Beckett wins the Nobel Prize. Returning to "this cold city Paris," he tells a friend "It's gone quiet around me." He travels to Stuttgart to read at a Hölderlin celebration. German listeners reject his clipped, cryptic lyrics—in one poem the lines seem symptomatic: "Yet we could not / darken over to you." During a small seminar in Freiburg, he actually reproaches Heidegger for inattentiveness. Later: "Celan is sick—incurable," says the philosopher who'd claimed that "Being speaks German."

Stehend! reads a one-word postcard to Gisèle from that German sojourn: "Standing fast," "Holding firm." Celan's last poem to his wife has a messianic ring:

> There will be something, soon now,
> that brims full with you
> and lifts up
> toward a mouth
> Out of a shardstrewn
> craze
> I stand up
> and look upon my hand,
> how it draws the one
> and only
> circle

Late March 1970: Celan declines to go along and meet Beckett. At the ENS he has students translating Kafka's "The Hunter Gracchus": "No one will read what I write here, no one will come to help me.... My ship is rudderless, it's driven by the wind blowing into the nethermost regions of death." On April 12th he writes again to Israel, quoting Kafka's diary: "But happiness only if I can raise the world into the Pure, the True, the Immutable."

April 13: What will be Celan's last poem turns to words he'd always kept by him: "dig...dark...hour...deep...open...stone...eye...you... read," and closes in quiet anticipation:

the Open ones carry
the stone behind their eye,
it knows you,
am Sabbath,

"on the Sabbath"—or perhaps, "come the Sabbath."

April 16: He tells his 14-year-old son Eric he can't after all take him
the next day, as planned, to a performance of *Godot*. Two tickets are
later found in his wallet.

April 19: Reading a biography of Hölderlin, Celan underlines these
words about his great mad predecessor: "Sometimes this genius goes
dark and sinks down into the bitter well of his heart." He does not (I
noticed when I came on this book in his library) underline the rest of
that sentence: "but mostly his apocalyptic star glitters wondrously."

April 19-20: Sometime during this night, Celan walks across from
Avenue Émile Zola to Apollinaire's darling Pont Mirabeau and
drowns in the Seine, though since his youth he's been a strong
swimmer. April 20th, eve of Pesach the festival of freedom, is also
Hitler's birthday.

May 1: Seven miles downstream a fisherman comes on Celan's body
caught in a filter of the river. Beckett's longtime German translator,
Elmar Tophoven, succeeds Celan as Reader in German at the École
Normale Supérieure.

Celan me dépasse, Samuel Beckett will later confide to a friend,
"Celan leaves me behind." But can that be so? Beckett, whom

everywhere you go in our mind you meet on his way back? Beckett's trilogy opens with a mother's death and ends with *The Unnamable*'s last words: "in the silence you don't know, you must go on, I can't go on, I'll go on."

Six years before his suicide by drowning, Paul Celan had written this poem:

WHERE?

At night in crumbling rockmass.
In trouble's rubble and scree,
in slowest tumult,
the wisdom-pit named Never.
Water needles
stitch up the split
shadow—it fights its way
deeper down,
free.

Since "shadow" is masculine in German, maybe those final lines are saying, "he fights his way / deeper down, / free."

THE BOOK OF LUAP NALEC

Pierre Joris

> *para mis Europeos*
> *para mis muertos*

> *We will never look very good*
> *We are too far gone on thought, and its rejections*
> *The two actions of a Noos*
> —Edward Dorn

> *Artistik ist der Versuch der Kunst, innerhalb des*
> *allgemeinen Verfalls der Inhalte sich selbst als Inhalt*
> *zu erleben und aus diesem Erlebnis einen neuen Stil*
> *zu bilden, es ist der Versuch, gegen den allgemeinen*
> *Nihilismus der Werte eine neue Transzendenz zu*
> *setzen: die Transzendenz der schöpferischen Lust...*

> *... im Grunde also meine ich, es gibt keinen anderen*
> *Gegenstand für die Lyrik als den Lyriker selbst.*
> —Gottfried Benn

1. THE BIRTH OF LUAP NALEC

(...)

224

somewhere a door closes.
I am not awake
alone . I am

thinking of
you, lady
la nuit américaine
I'm thinking

the strong body of America arched
night over an ephectic Europe

' e n t r o p o c e p h a l u s'

God's peace, Benn, would have that coin
(age that knew the brain's skin
Roman des Phänotyp:
played Doktor
wrote Morgue
dies)

Celan dares
go further, *Faden*
sun through
threadbare
web,
his breath

turned

to water.

How dare you
dare?
                    Face
myself
past the bright
wound mirror?
                    Stare
where you
single counter-
swimmer
count
        &
            break
the floated
spines,
the lines.

            Time
broke us
in,
    saddled us
with a sadness
(post-modern, no,

post-mortem) its
vigor the rigor
of water now
frozen, the white
silenced sheet,
Pleistocene

place I search
to find
the shifted
stance.

Sight threads sense shreds
from the folded image knit
behind time:
                    invisible enough
to see you, you came
through all the walls
you came turncoat eye

eye turned
inside out
of which
I see

Scintillation of
my she break
the thin
film
        the ice-white
skin
        an angled slit
reverses where
we were.
            are.
                    From where
                (here & there)

SPRECHGITTER

I
the shifter, am spoken
through
these chambers -
a quartering
of words
             badly bruised
             & water-logged
but I must keep
on talking keep
calling

your name
changling, maiden

what is
your name
what is is
shimmers, stammers
on the vocal-cords-bridge, in the
Great Inbetween
with all that has room in it
even without speech?

Antara   you call

yourself there
Lady of the Gate

& here
        Gate
of the Lady
          through
which Nalec
lately hither-
silenced,
alived
despite all
by the breath of
the shifting ice.

Out of a dream of drowning
the drowning,
of a dream the contra-
script
read us into meeting
in the Serpentcoach
takes us
        once past
your white cypress
through the cypher-
wall.

        Thus break the ice
to know.
Though we had met
before it had been
I
in you
from birthseed

out, til now when
I in you
is
Nalec
whom open
you enter
now through him
at last
　　　　　you climb
in me
up the dark
memory shaft
　　　　　　　you climb
to the day.

Light entered me
lit the walls
of the cave
I was. A fistful
of consonants
drifts from mouth to
mouth, in-
ward
　　　　　the lightbeams
dance them
wall-
　　　　　word where
the vowels wait
obedient to the light
where
syllable by syllable

the loud heartthread
is trembled
clear.
          Your voice
Antara
declares itself -
I begin
to witness
at the end

of a long day

done . done . done .

2. *AFTER DONE TRYING TO WAKE HER UP*

merciless

we go by
sound alone.

bark back:
at the end
was the word.

He said it is done.

Thrice reaped
the long day's
echo

/ing

        . done .

            in)

&

Luap Nalec
rose, stood
against the end.
We no longer go by
but stay, cowering
erring
        haunched

nostrils flare for
the reaped echo's
shell turns
to earth.

the earth turns
to mire
      & mirth
          & myrrh.

ends smell
of dung, of
things done in

thus now the newly
sounded smells stir
the small grey earths
make possible:

matters like take
a tree's dead trunk
a word to be dug out
a will comes in
we fire-hollow
the vowelled belly
then sand the ends
arched consonants
down to firm
mirror-roundness

Roll on . From here
uphill. Go. OVERland. OVERnight. Nearby. Here
HEAR space beckons now the boats now the place beckons
the readymade the signed objects / singed subject this old
construct continent renamed renamable.

            Singing the singed parts.

The burned offerings
up up in flames
putrify the hard chains
purify the heart claims.

A wide-on she says I have a wide-on for Europe
I am she & you singer I have a soft spot for you
Antara make me fucker give me rope
enough to know your face the whole
length I'll sing it now

:
that the links be made
visible again
I'll weave a meshless
net of space
you are the song
are the loom
I am the breath
turns & spins
the yarn
anew.

HYMEN: I) fr. GK *hymen* wedding song, fr. *Hymen* God of marriage (lit. a wedding cry); perhaps akin to GK *hymnos* hymn, song of praise.

    1) *archaic* : marriage
    2) *archaic* : a wedding song

    II) fr. GK *hymen* membrane, caul (perhaps akin to SK *syuman* band, thong):

    a fold of mucuous membrane partly closing the orifice of the vagina.

SYU-: To bind, sew.

    Variant form *su-*; OE *seam* seam.
    Suffixed from *su-tro-*: in SK *sutra*, thread, string.
    Suffixed shortened from *su-men* : in GK *hymen* thin skin membrane.

_____

235

Das Gedicht behauptet sich am Rande seiner selbst; es ruft und holt sich, um bestehen zu können, unausgesetzt aus seinem Schon-nicht-mehr in sein Immer-noch zurück.

Paul Celan

La scène n'illustre que l'idée, pas une action effective, dans un hymen (d'où procède le rêve), vicieux mais sacré, entre le désir et l'accomplissement, la perpétration et son souvenir: ici devançant, là remémorant, au futur, au passé, sous une apparence fausse de présent. Tel opère le Mime, dont le jeu se borne à une allusion perpétuelle sans briser la glace: il installe, ainsi, un milieu pur, de fiction.

Stéphane Mallarmé

———————————————

Mal tu par l'encre même

Stéphane Mallarmé

Et me détacher de l'idée de l'être est-ce en faire un ou se tenir toujours en dehors? Je crois que c'est se tenir en dehors dedans, en y étant, et y être ce n'est pas se tenir au-dessus du Mal mais *dedans* et être le Mal lui-même, le Mal qu'il y ait Dieu à rassasier, l'hymen de la Morgue qui est que le pli ne fut jamais un pli...

Antonin Artaud

236

TYMPAN: 1a: drum

b: a celtic bowed stringed musical instrument

2a: (obs.) TYMPANUM

b: any of various membranous plates functioning basically
like the membranous tympanum of the ear.

3a: *or* TYMPAN SHEET: a sheet of material (as paper or cloth) in
a printing press that is placed between the impression surface and the
paper to be printed.

TYMPANUM: The tense double membrane seperating the outer from the
middle ear - tympanic membrane - called also eardrum.

A membrane in a sound producing organ that acts as a
resonator.

TYMPANIC NERVE: a branch of the glossopharyngeal nerve arising from the
petrosal ganglion, distributed to the walls of the
tympanum of the ear where it takes part in forming a plexus.

237

III. THE NEWT LIFE

> *Mas per melhs assire*
> *mon chan,*
> *vau cercan*
> *bos motz en fre*
> *que son tuir cargat e ple*
> *d'us estranhs sens naturals;*
> *mas no sabon tuich de cals.*
> —Guiraut de Bornelh

Dee-doo, dee-dum.

No such thing
as a simple twist

Dee-da, dee-doo,
"What is it stammers
under the lintels of words

a breath of air"
Dee . Die .
        Die Dame Art
Amiss
       echoes of
hilaritas
(common salt
added to
the rarer gold
of *cars rimas*)
& never sad

thus spoke
the shuffled
words of cause.

         Re : birth
breath-sound
of the sun
coming
in the maiden.

                (the given
Doors
         tympan & hymen
oblique boundaries
of sound
        &,
          hammer-
headedness) the

"asunderwritten"
on the made bed
of fall or
fall's ore
         (gold) aurora
l'aura,
        autumn's *Atem* a
         breath
         breaking
on the unmade bed
        through
        taking

summer's hymn, her
maiden:
           had . done for .
          taking
it all in
to
   where
a newt life beckons.

Sap.
   Filling the gaps
my hollowed teeth & I
the cranky lion.
Lie low, sweet form.

Come again, come
fill her, ful-
fill the prostrate
prophecy.
          A
proferred apple that
won't bite
you who are
at this late twist re-
turned
from rust
to lust
         (a verb
to dare win/ter
: thrice strapped
to the must

you miss
the music our
lion's share.

　　　　Miss
the false air, *l'aura*
of pestilence,
etiological clouds
to be seeded
in a different
city.

Dee-doo, dee-dum,
no such thing
as a simple twist.

　　　　In the middle
of the newt life
　　　　　　winter
won over
time now time
enough to
choose & leave
a language
where
　　　　"verb"
is a noun &
eye means
verge
　　　　or urge
　　　　a verge

cannot come
to mean.

IV. THE EAR

Strapped & sealed
he missed the music.
The spoils

for greed of which
the crew goes overboard
harvests nothing
but the languish of fishes.
Fool's gold
lure of *Muspelheim,*
shiny coin your
face rubbed out rubbed
down to the blank
stare of the sea's
surface.

While the stultified
ship shuttles on
we follow its course
with eyes strained
no line links it
to a loom it drifts
with masts sung earthward
set free in a space
where right side up

& upside down
no longer mean
it weaves along
not ship not church
a shapeless shape.

Protected
by his hymened
tympanum
no longer
divided
in his attentions
- impregnable fortress -
the lion
listens,
                    hears
the gyroscope
the only function
of his organ.

Strapped
to his stirrups
he swings
a hammer sounding
the walls.
                    Follows
the echo's
threads &
careful not to
lean against
the shaky ramps

begins to explore
the beginnings of
his story.

        Tympanum . Labyrinth . Hymen . Thread .

Advancing now
(standing
         walking
            dancing)
wrapped into
he moves
enveloped never
to emerge again
the form of an ear
built around a dam
turning about
its internal wall.

Newt shape
of a city
he feels along
(a labyrinth
semi-circular canals
- semi-lunar)
          a city
wrapped
like a snail
around a floodgate
a dam
       stretching

towards the sea, closed
in upon itself
but open towards
the sea.

        Amazed
the lion finds
himself
on a beach
he bends down
to the other form
the female form
picks up
what the sea
spelled out a
shell
        full &
emptied of its
waters
        anamnesis
of the sea's ear
the only sound
against
his ear.

        It happens
has to happen
here . the crack
resounds
        birth
of a language

245

a different song
"sexual jubilation
is a glottal choice of
a lunar canal
the clear auricular ringing
a clear instillation of
sound"

          cracks
the wax seal
cuts the straps
           release
& the storm
abides.

THE DEATH OF CELAN

Yehuda Amichai

I heard about it in London.
They said he killed himself.

The same rope
was tugging lightly at my neck.
But it wasn't a rope: he
died by water.
The same water, water, water.

Last metaphor:
a life like a death.
(The same water, water, water.)

translated from the Hebrew by Harold Schimmel

A NOTE ON THE DEATH OF PAUL CELAN

Clayton Eshleman

While living in Sherman Oaks, California, in the spring of 1970, I had the following dream: a man that I recognized as Paul Celan walked to the bank of the Seine in Paris and stepped up onto a stone which I also recognized as the "Vallejo stone." Celan stood there for a moment—then leapt into the river.

When I mentioned my dream to someone a week or so later, I was informed that the poet had just drowned in the Seine, an apparent suicide.

The "Vallejo stone" refers to a poem that César Vallejo wrote while living in Paris in the mid-1930s. Like many of the poems that Vallejo wrote during these years, "Parado en una piedra" records his acute sensitivity to human suffering. This particular poem strikes me as a stay against suicide. In the early 1930s, Vallejo still believed that a Communist-inspired world revolution would occur, but this belief was beginning to founder, overwhelmed by the suffering he found everywhere daily.

Vallejo's untitled poem opens with the following two stanzas:

> Idle on a stone,
> unemployed,
> scroungy, horrifying,
> at the bank of the Seine, it comes and goes.
> Conscience then sprouts from the river,
> with petiole and outlines of the greedy tree;
> from the river the city rises and falls, made of
>   embraced wolves.

The idle one sees it coming and going,
monumental, carrying his fasts in his concave
    head,
on his chest his purest lice
and below
his little sound, that of his pelvis,
silent between two big decisions,
and below,
further down,
a paperscrap, a nail, a match . . .

Bottom thoughts. The generational body, out of work, ends in the trash in the Seine's slime.

I think of this "Vallejo stone" as a locus of exile where lamentation is tested. It brings to mind a passage from Rilke's 10th *Duino Elegy* that evokes the crisis of lamentation for the twentieth century. A young woman, identified as a Lament, responds to a young man's questions, saying:

We were a great clan, once, we Laments. Our fathers
worked the mines in that mountain range. Sometimes
you'll find a polished lump of ancient sorrow among men
or petrified rage from the slag of some old volcano.
Yes, that came from there. We used to be rich.

Attempting to read my dream in the penumbra of Vallejo's and Celan's lives and poetries, I see that Vallejo, still weighted with some of the riches of lamentation, could address the misery of humankind from his stone, and then walk away from the Seine to write other poems.

249

For Celan, both of whose parents were murdered in Nazi death camps, lamentation was not entirely empty but was so distorted by the absurdity of praising anything that its so-called riches had been undermined. I suspect that at a certain point he could no longer even feel sorry for himself.

From *Sprachgitter* (1959) onward, the movements of words and lines in Celan's poetry have a strong, twisting, downward propulsion, like strands of a rope that is, at the same time, tightening with increasing weight *and* self-destructing through torsion into cast free strands. As if the direction is vertically commanded by a central suck, a whirlpool. Language as spars, rapidly milling. For example (in Cid Corman's translation from "The Syllable Ache," a poem in *Die Niemandrose*, 1964):

Forgotten grabbed
at To-be-forgotten, earthparts, heartparts
swam,
sank and swam. Columbus
the time-
less in eye, the mother-
flower,
murdered masts and sails. All fares forth,
free,
discovering,
the compass-flower fades, point
by leafpoint to height and to day, in blacklight
of wildrudderstreaks. In coffins,
in urns, canopic jars
awoke the little children
Jasper, Agate, Amethyst—peoples,
stock and kin, a blind

Let there be

is knotted in
the serpentheaded free-
ropes—:

By modifying "Let there be" with "blind," freedom and license
twist into each other, and for a moment Aleister Crowley's "Do
What Thou Wilt" shows its lust-deformed face. By putting it that
way I attempt to indicate to what an extent Celan's poetry contains
a pronouncement of creation emptied of meaning. When "Do What
Thou Wilt" becomes, as it does for Crowley, the only law, there is no
meaningful creation. The god-spark is exterminated, one is no one,
one says one's prayer to ashes.

On another level, Celan's contraries were "I" and "Thou,"
and in his mature poetry they grow unbearably close, closer than
contraries can to function; one could say they devour each other,
the living become the dead, the dead the living, and out of such
devastation a grand but dreadful vista opens. Celan's voice is finally
consumed in a "we" that is the living and the dead scratching a
message on stone to "no one." Under the stress of such an anti-
vision, nothing is forgotten: memories of the death camps and
insignificant slights have hundreds of doors opening on each other. It
is a condition in which there cannot be poetry *and* in which there can
only be poetry.

In regarding Paul Celan today, I meditate on the stamina
of his wound. He neither allowed it to flow at full vent, nor did he
brilliantly cicatrize it at the right hour. He worked it as a muscle as
long as there was any strength left in it—he knelt at its altar alone,

and thus did not set other energies in motion that might have given him reasons to continue to live at the point that the wound ceased to ache.

Then there was only numbness. And a great poetic testimony in which Paul Celan and annihilated millions can be sensed as a single "we" that you and I can try to pronounce.

[Los Angeles, 1975]

PETRIFIED

Fanny Howe

She went to a hotel where she knew there were windows that would open. There was also a balcony. It was cement and only three feet wide. She stepped out to glance down at the tiny trail of automobiles fifty floors below, when someone slid shut the glass door behind her. She didn't know who. She couldn't open the door. She beat on it again and again and no one came. She didn't dare look down. She lay on the ground and called. She cried. But no one knew she was there. No one could hear her. It could be days, weeks, forever before she was found. If she got back inside, she would be where she was before. The rooms and doors and floors would unfold with her movements in them. If she stayed where she was, she would gradually starve and fail. She would probably stay in a fetal curl. She would probably watch the clouds and stars. She would be aware of the beauty they held, and begin to study them. She would whisper to some being unknown to all, once she realized her calls would never be heard. She would be in the situation of paralysis that is familiar to us all. Not given admittance in any direction. Like the unborn.

"It is time the stone made an effort to flower."
—Paul Celan

"DEEP IN THE GLOWING TEXT-VOID": TRANSLATING LATE CELAN

John Felstiner

One of Paul Celan's latest, briefest poems, written back in Paris after his long-deferred 1969 journey to Israel, closes with an imperative to its author or reader—

> hör dich ein
> mit dem Mund

—an imperative that in subtly resisting translation also seems destined for the poem's translator.[1] The verb here, *hör dich ein,* did not previously exist in German; this poem has formed it. So we struggle for an equivalent. The English "listen in" and "tune in" are inexact; "hear yourself in / with the mouth," though literally correct, loses the threefold pulse of the German. A French version says "insouffle-toi l'écoute," "blow in" (or "inspirit") "your listening"—a bold but maybe excessive figure of Godlike resuscitation.[2] Because the verb in Celan's poem demands an attentiveness that turns into responsiveness, the self given up yet given, perhaps I can catch this urgency with a slight sound play (and rhythmic overlay) on "hör dich ein / mit dem Mund":

> hear deep in
> with your mouth.

---

1   Paul Celan. *Gesammelte Werke,* ed. Beda Allemann & Stefan Reichert, with Rolf Bücher, 5 vols. (Frankfurt, 1983), 3:104. This collected edition (*GW*) is hereafter cited in the text by volume and page number. See also John Felstiner, "Translating Paul Celan's 'Jerusalem' Poems," *Religion and Literature* 16:1 (Winter 1984), 37-47.

2   Paul Celan, *Enclos du temps: Zeitgehöft,* trans. Martine Broda (Paris, 1985).

Can we overhear these final lines evoking a translator's activity, a thoroughgoing audition that in turn commits one to speech?

The kind of hearing called for in translating this poem can start a to-and-fro process of reciprocal discovery—interpretation abetting translation while at the same time the not-yet-adequate rendering of a line will push toward some further sense in it. Here then is the German poem, "Die Posaunenstelle," from 16 November 1969, with my version of it:

DIE POSAUNENSTELLE	THE TRUMPETS' PLACE
tief im glühenden	deep in the glowing
Leertext,	empty-text,
in Fackelhöhe,	at torch height,
im Zeitloch:	in the timehole:
hör dich ein	hear deep in
mit dem Mund.	with your mouth.

Everything until the colon and verse break has been (without any verb) delineating a place, so that someone can then be told "hör dich ein / mit dem Mund." This place—is it "the trumpets' place," or is it "deep in the glowing / empty-text," or "at torch height," or "in the timehole"? More likely it is all of them conflated; to identify it took citing all five lines. And this place is, at the same time, Celan's verse itself, about which the closing lines urge you to "hear deep in / with your mouth."

Celan's German, to be truly heard, comes particularly in need of translating because of its obscurity. His major speech "The Meridian" (1960) defends "the darkness attaching to poetry, for the sake of an encounter, from its—perhaps self-devised—distance or strangeness" (3:195). In this brief lyric "Die Posaunenstelle," Celan's phrasings seem only half-emerged from shadow, "rearward-spoken" (to quote a 1967 poem; 2:312) or as if rawly translated from some lost tongue into German and needing further translation even for native speakers. So tracing this lyric through a process of translation may prove a more than usually revealing task.

For the first line and title, "Die Posaunenstelle," English versions say "The trumpet part," "The trumpet's part,"[3] and a French translation has "Le passage des trompettes," quite reasonably taking *Stelle* as the "place" in a book or musical score. But what place, in what book? Citing Martin Luther's use of the word *Posaunen* to translate the apocalyptic "trumpets" sounded by seven angels, the Swiss scholar Bernhard Böschenstein definitively ties Celan's lyric to Revelation 8: "And the third angel sounded, and there fell from heaven a great star, burning as a torch" ("torch" is *Fackel,* as in Celan's poem).[4] Certainly such Christian figurings of Yahweh's destructive, revelatory wrath may stand behind this poem, which echoes Luther and, like the biblical passage, starkly juxtaposes height and depth. But a very different "place," I believe, lies closer to the genesis of "Die Posaunenstelle" and bears upon the way a translation will interpret the poem.

Celan's 1969 journey to Israel had been anticipated for some time, probably most strongly after the Six Day War. During that first week of June 1967, when Israeli troops regained the Old City of Jerusalem, he wrote a poem entitled "Denk dir":

3   Paul Celan, *Poems,* trans. Michael Hamburger (New York, 1988), 342; Celan, "The Second Cycle of *Zeitgehöft,*" trans. Pierre Joris, *Sulfur* 11 (1984), 21.

4   Bernhard Böschenstein, "Erste Notizen zu Celans letzten Gedichten," in *Text u. Kritik* 53-54 (1977; 2nd ed., July 1984), 63. Another version of this essay appears in Martine Broda, ed., *Contre-jour: Études sur Paul Celan* (Paris, 1986). *Posaune* in German denotes a trombone as well as a trumpet.

Just think:
the peat-bog soldier of Masada
makes a home for himself...
Just think: your
own hand
has held this
piece
of habitable earth
again suffered up
into life.
Just think:
that came toward me,
name-awake, hand-awake
for ever,
from the unburiable.
                    (2:227)

When Celan reached Jerusalem in October 1969, he walked around
the Old City; its gates, especially, figure in several poems he wrote
right afterwards. In one poem he formed the word *Tempeltiefen,*
"Temple-depths," connoting the ancient city along with what no
longer exists there. And a poem composed several days after "Die
Posaunenstelle" has as its central line "sag, dass Jerusalem i s t,"
"say, that Jerusalem i s" (3:105)—an assertion, or rather a call
for assertion, that sounds both hopeful and desperate. Israel, for a
survivor who in 1948 had written to relatives there, "Perhaps I am
one of the last who must live out to the end the destiny of the Jewish
spirit in Europe";[5] Israel, for a poet with nothing left but the German

---

5   Paul Celan, letter of 2 August 1948, quoted in Bianca Rosenthal, "Quellen zum
frühen Celan," *Monatshefte* 75:4 (1983), 403.

mother tongue rooting him in a Diaspora matrix; Israel, for Paul Celan, held out a redemptive promise he doubted he could grasp.

Very shortly before Celan's visit, the Israeli archaeologist Benjamin Mazar had made a remarkable find at the Temple Mount in Jerusalem: a large hewn stone lying below the southwest corner on the Herodian pavement, toppled from a parapet when the Romans destroyed the Second Temple.[6] Incised on this ashlar are the words העיקתה תיבל‎, l'veit ha-tekiah, "to the place [or house] of trumpeting" or "the place of the shofar blast." Josephus (*The Jewish War*, 4:582) mentions such a tower, where the priest would blow a trumpet to signal the beginning and end of the Sabbath, and the Mishnah (Sukka 5.5) confirms that the shofar was sounded in the temple for daily ritual, Sabbath, and festivals. The find of "beit ha-tekiah" at the Western Wall, announced in 1969, excited interest because it marked the temple's flourishing and also its destruction.

To ascribe "Die Posaunenstelle" to the Revelation of Saint John, then, preempts this other possible "place of trumpeting," once located high on the temple above the busiest corner in Jerusalem. Something "unburiable," something "again suffered up / into life," to cite Celan's June 1967 poem, emerged with an incised stone "deep... in the timehole."

Now as it happens, I have heard recently from a friend who showed Paul Celan around Jerusalem in October 1969. "Keine Ausgrabungen, bitte!" Celan said then, "Please, no excavations!" (And one wonders why not—the heat, the dust, the tedium, something else?). If in fact he did not ever see or learn of the incised stone, that makes its pertinence to his poem all the more arresting.

---

6   Benjamin Mazar, *The Mountain of the Lord: Excavating Jerusalem* (New York, 1975), 138. I am grateful to Bill Daleski for relaying this datum, noted by Adam Mendilow in connection with Celan's poem. The stone is now in the Israel Museum, Jerusalem.

What if, some time after writing "Die Posaunenstelle," he had seen a description of the stone? Often Celan while reading—I know this from the margins of books he owned and from his letters—would encounter some piece of fact, a detail from Judaic lore, say, or from Nietzsche or Kafka, and this item would suddenly, gratifyingly tally with something he himself had already written. For instance in 1959, Celan came upon a sentence by Walter Benjamin that identifies Kafka's characters as having "lost their house of prayer...lost the Holy Writ,"[7] and he penciled in the margin, "vgl. Mandelstamm, 'Sie, die nicht mehr priesterlichen'" ("cf. Mandelshtam, 'They, no longer priestly'")—that is, he recalled the German verse from an Osip Mandelshtam poem he had translated the year before (5:95). Evidently some trace of sacral loss passed from Kafka through Benjamin and Mandelshtam to Celan. Such coincidences he liked to call "meridians" because they brought a far-flung circle home; they linked him up, confirming his all-too-precarious sense of participation in an ongoing tradition. The stone inscribed "to the place of trumpeting," then, may be not simply a source but an ever-present corroboration of Celan's figurative insight.

We can also "hear deep in" to another, fundamental text beneath "Die Posaunenstelle." The word *Posaune* itself entered the German language in Luther's New and Old Testament translations, in Revelation, Matthew, Psalms, and elsewhere. In fact Luther used it at the first biblical occurrence of the Hebrew term *shofar,* a ram's horn, in Exodus.[8] Just before the giving of the Ten Commandments, there

---

7   Walter Benjamin, "Franz Kafka," in *Schriften,* ed. Theodor W. & Gretel Adorno, 2 vols. (Frankfurt, 1955), 2:228; also in Benjamin, *Illuminations,* ed. Hannah Arendt, trans. Harry Zohn (New York, 1969), 139.

8   Luther's first Bible translations were of some psalms, none of them containing the word *shofar.* Then he translated the New Testament. So the very first occurrence of *Posaune* in German is probably in Matthew 24:31, rendering the Greek *salpinx*—

is thunder and lightning "and the voice of shofar exceeding loud," and the Lord coming down in fire on Sinai and smoke rising and the mountain quaking, "and the voice of the shofar grew louder and louder" (Exod. 19.6). Then just after God speaks the commandments, the people feel thunder and *lapidim,* a Hebrew word the Buber-Rosenzweig Bible renders as *Fackeln* ("torches"), and again the people hear the voice of the shofar—*Posaune,* as translated by both Luther and Buber-Rosenzweig.[9] This Revelation, at Sinai, or at least the biblical passage recounting it, stands deeply if not immediately behind Celan's "Posaunenstelle."[10]

Celan's option of the word *Posaune* to enter both "text" and "time" inevitably takes him by way of Luther's German. How might Luther's presence affect a Jew writing after the *Nullpunkt,* the null point or zero degree at which German literature found itself in May 1945? It is partly Luther's virulent anti-Semitism, but mainly the

---

the same word the Septuagint had used for *shofar* in Exodus. Shortly afterwards, Luther translated the Old Testament, now using *Posaune* for the Hebrew *shofar.*

9   The word *Fackeln* appears at this point in the 1954 edition of the Buber-Rosenzweig translation. In the first edition, the word used is *Brände.*

10   Stéphane Mosès relates "Die Posaunenstelle" to Exodus and other Hebraic sources in an excellent essay, "Paul Celan: Die Posaunenstelle," in *Spuren der Schrift: Von Goethe bis Celan* (Frankfurt, 1987), 134-50; English version in Sanford Budick & Wolfgang Iser, eds., *Languages of the Unsayable: The Play of Negativity in Literature and Literary Theory* (New York, 1989), 209-24. Otto Pöggeler also discusses Celan's poem in "Sein und Nichts: Mystische Elemente bei Heidegger und Celan," in Wolfgang Böhme, ed., *Zu dir hin: Über mystische Lebenserfahrung von Meister Eckhart bis Paul Celan* (Frankfurt, 1987), 291-93. He refers the poem to the Revelation at Sinai, making no mention of the New Testament book of Revelation. He notes quite suggestively that when Israeli troops reached the Western Wall in Jerusalem in June 1967, the army's chief rabbi blew the shofar there. And in a one-sentence parenthesis, Pöggeler says that at excavations near the wall "a stone was found, showing that already in ancient times the shofar was blown here."

profound influence his Bible translation had on German language and literature that complicates the way "Die Posaunenstelle" sends a taproot to Hebraic sources. After all, in bringing his Old Testament closer than Saint Jerome's to the Hebrew original, Luther hoped this vernacular Scripture would not only draw Germans but convert Jews to a reformed Christianity. When Franz Rosenzweig began translating Hebrew hymns and liturgy into German, he remarked to Gershom Scholem that Luther had Christianized the German language.[11] Yet Celan's access to the Hebrew Bible was not necessarily mediated by Luther. He once read a Hugo Bergmann essay on the sanctification of God's name in Judaism, where Bergmann cites a key verse from Leviticus in German (and not, incidentally, in Luther's German), Celan in a fluent hand has marginally added the Hebrew text.[12] So an ostensibly Lutheran term such as *Posaune* may show Celan not accepting but implicating a certain tradition.

Even more to the point, Celan knew in his very being (think of the harrow in Kafka's "Penal Colony") what brutal compromising his mother tongue underwent centuries after Luther. So he inscribed that knowledge into his own verse, sometimes exposing and sometimes purging a German language that throughout Nazi Europe had "passed through the thousand darknesses of deathbringing speech," as he put it (3:186). One lyric of his on Jerusalem quotes Isaiah in Meister Eckhart's medieval German, as if forestalling

---

11 Franz Rosenzweig to Gershom Scholem, 10 March 1921, in Rosenzweig, *Briefe und Tagebücher,* vol. 2, *1918-1929,* ed. Rachel Rosenzweig & Edith Rosenzweig Scheinmann (The Hague, 1979), 698; also in *Franz Rosenzweig: His Life and Thought,* ed. Nahum N. Glatzer (New York, 1961), 100-101.

12 Hugo Bergmann, "Die Heiligung des Namens," in *Vom Judentum: Ein Sammelbuch,* ed. Hans Kohn (Leipzig, 1913), 22.

even Luther, and then goes back further to the (transliterated) Hebrew itself.[13] Certainly the German language came to Celan as reconstituted by Luther (and it also came, for him especially, inspirited by Hölderlin and Heidegger). The word *Posaune* must point "deep," I think, so as to reconstitute Luther's German, to reach through the Reformation toward a more original constitution, a founding text somehow both glowing and empty.

Yet another "Old Testament" source may come to mind, again from a pre-Christian apocalyptic moment. That the Revelation of Saint John specifies seven angels and trumpets can make it seem especially pertinent to Celan's (seven-line) poem, because of the number seven's eschatological significance for him (1:52, 83; 3:172). But it would prove even more pertinent to remember the book of Joshua (6.3), where seven priests bear seven shofars (*Posaunen*) before the Ark of the Covenant, circling the city of Jericho seven times; and to remember that "when the people heard the sound of the horn" they literally shouted themselves into the promised land.

Why not, after all, try translating the title line of "Die Posaunenstelle" as "The Place of the Shofar"? On that fallen stone, the word *tekiah* literally means "blast" and designates the blowing of the shofar at the New Year's Day and Day of Atonement services as well as on the Sabbath; for the Jubilee year the shofar is also sounded, and it will usher in the messianic age. Indeed the Hebrew term itself, *tekiah,* occurs with some salience in a 1962 poem by Celan:

> ...a ram's horn lifts you
> —*Tekiah!*—
> like a trumpet blast above and beyond the nights into day.

---

13   *GW,* 2:327. See John Felstiner, "Translating Paul Celan's 'Du sei wie du,'" *Prooftexts* 6:2 (1986), 172-83.

(1:285)

Here Celan's German is *Widderhorn* ("ram's horn") and
Posaunenschall, usually rendered as "trumpet blast." So in
translating the later poem "Die Posaunenstelle," "shofar" would
sound a most particular note—whether unduly or not depends, as so
often with Celan, on how strongly the strain of Jewishness may be
felt within his writing.

Especially those poems written immediately after Celan's
brief stay in Israel come ridden with ambivalence and riven textually
by ambiguity as to how the promised land, and its revived tongue
might possibly house a poet "when he is a Jew and the language of
his poems is German," as he said in an August 1948 letter to relatives
in the new state of Israel. Although Celan was strongly drawn to
the books of Isaiah and Jeremiah, and in 1967 ended a poem on
Jerusalem with the Hebrew from Isaiah, *kumi ori,* "Arise, shine" (Isa.
60.1), nonetheless the redemptive energy those scriptures sometimes
lend his verse never appears unconflicted. Glowing deep within "Die
Posaunenstelle," for instance, it would be heartening to locate this
text from Isaiah: "And it shall come to pass on that day, that a great
shofar shall be blown, and they shall come that were lost in the land
of Assyria, and outcasts in the land of Egypt, and shall worship the
Lord on the holy mountain in Jerusalem" (27.13). But Celan's lines
can hardly ring with such prophetic certainty of an ingathering from
exile.

To find the "trumpet place" *tief im glühenden / Leertext*
suggests that what's "deep" in some empty-text is at once
fundamental and yet profoundly inaccessible. Celan wrote a poem
the week before "Die Posaunenstelle" that situatues itself outside the
walls of Jerusalem's Old City and that turns on an archaeological
figure of richness and danger:

a goldbuoy, from
Temple-depths,
marked the danger that
stilly succumbed to us.
       (3:100)

And the last thing he composed, shortly before drowning himself in
the Seine in 1970, begins this way:

Vinegrowers dig up
the darkhoured clock,
deep upon deep.
       (3:123)

Such excavation could turn up death or produce new life, and most
likely it must do both—"Do not sunder No from Yes," Celan wrote
in 1954, "He speaks true who speaks shadow" (1:135).

Sited "deep" in a text, the place of the trumpet or shofar
seems a source beyond our grasp—both essential and alien, which
is the double valence attaching to Celan's most telling formulations.
"Whoever walks on his head has heaven as an abyss beneath him"
(3:195): Celan's "Meridian" speech makes this a figure for poetic
and spiritual liberation, precisely because of its terrifying paradox.

The same holds for "glühenden / Leertext," which the line
break splices "glowing / empty," like the line break "at torch height,
/ in the timehole"—both breaks evidently spanning polar extremes.
How can a text be glowing and empty? To find that out, perhaps the
riddle needs rephrasing: What is a text when it is an empty-text?
Answer: the Bible. To begin with, Scripture itself originates in a
word spoken over emptiness: "The earth was unformed and void,

and darkness upon the face of the deep" (Luther has "Leer" for "void," "Tiefe" for "deep"): "And God said, 'Let there be light.'" What's more, by the very fact that Scripture asks to be fulfilled, in both a covenantal and a hermeneutic sense, we may call it "empty." The Bible forms an "empty-text" because once given the words of the *sh'ma,* with their opening imperative, "Hear, O Israel" or "Höre Israel," we are told to "teach them," "talk of them," and "write them" (Deut. 6.4). Taking it more strongly, I would now translate Celan's term *Leertext* as "text-void," making two equally stressed substantives: "text-void," a presence embedding an absence that wants filling, that glows with want, that wants response, repetition, exegesis, translation.

If as a listener you do "hear deep in / with your mouth," Celan's unprecedented compound *Leertext* will make a perfect homonym with *Lehrtext.* Now *Lehre* means "teaching," and so does the Hebrew word *Torah,* the Mosaic Law. That this poem should devote a line to pun on *Torah* as "empty-text" or "text-void" confirms an enigmatic sense of Judaic authority Celan had in common with Kafka, whose key parable "Before the Law" he once translated into Romanian.[14] In that parable the seeker never gains entrance, but before dying he sees something like a glowing text-void, a radiance streaming inextinguishably from the open door of the Law.

What Kafka before the war uncannily anticipated, Celan's writing bears literal witness to: an all-but-inaccessible Revelation, a near-eclipse of the Word, a "frightful muting" (3:186). Thus a 1957 lyric called "Flower," marking the first word Celan's son spoke, calls it "a blindman's word" and greets the event in precariously creational

---

14   See John Felstiner, "Kafka and the Golem: Translating Paul Celan," *Prooftexts* 6:2 (1986), 172-83.

terms: "we scooped the darkness empty, we found / the word" (1:164). Another 1957 poem, whose title "In Mundhöhe" ("At Mouth Height") joins two terms from "Die Posaunenstelle," ends less expectantly than the late poem: "Lip knew. Lip knows. / Lip mutes it at the last" (1:180). And another poem from that year coins the term *schriftleer,* "empty of writing" or "Scripture-devoid" (1:169). Often the word *leer* works paradoxically, as in "Mandorla" (1961), when it embodies a kabbalist conception of divine nothingness: "Empty almond, kingly blue" (1:244); or in a later poem, when "the blown- / empty lung / blossoms" (2:42).

Yet another cryptic term hovers near the surface of Celan's poem, a term his first and third lines together almost pronounce: *Leerstelle,* meaning "vacant space." This unusual word actually does occur in the one piece of prose fiction he wrote, "Conversation in the Mountains" (1959), where two Jews meet on an alpine road one evening when "the sun, and not only that, had gone down."[15] They talk about various things, including speech itself and a "No-One" who never answers. At one point they stand there silent, but "it's merely a pause, it's a word-gap, it's a vacant space [*eine Leerstelle*], you can see the syllables all standing around." Celan's "Conversation" displays the tenuous state of communicative, meaningful language in a world rendered alien to these babblers. In "Die Posaunenstelle," the virtual presence of *Leerstelle* may also involve its grammatical sense—a place opened up in a sentence and needing to be filled. Even the least sort of "text-void," for a poet as stretched as Celan, can have immense consequence.

Does Holy Scripture constitute only a *Leertext* after "that which happened" (3:186), as Celan called what we call Holocaust or Shoah? "Psalm," for instance, voices an emptied teaching, "Blessed

---

15   *GW,* 3:169-173. See John Felstiner, "'Goodbye Silence': Paul Celan's 'Conversation in the Mountains," *Stanford Humanities Review* 1:1 (Spring 1989), 33-43.

art thou, No One" (1:225), a rupture of the ritual benediction. Still, where a text remains to recur to, recourse becomes resource: the "text-void" glows, however brokenly refuted. So it matters which Scripture we hear within "Die Posaunenstelle." Referring this poem to the Book of Revelation, as do several critics,[16] ought also to mean specifying Christianity's complicity in the event that darkens Celan's lyric voice. His word *Fackelhöhe*, "torch height," may indeed evoke Saint John's angel blowing a trumpet, and the star falling from heaven like a torch to destroy the world. But this apocalyptic vision cannot enhance, it must embitter, a poem whose heights and depths measure not only the range of theophany but also the extremities of a three-millennium civilization utterly threatened.

Those paradoxes framing "Die Posaunenstelle"—"glowing" and "empty," "height" and "hole"—also expose the radical paradox of composing in a German language that had "passed through the thousand darknesses of deathbringing speech" (3:186). Celan shared this blinding plight most closely with his friend Nelly Sachs, and perhaps her book *Glühende Rätsel* (1964), "Glowing Enigmas," lent to his poem an emanation of Jewish suffering. A similar strain can be felt in his fashioning of German words to make up this poem's topography: *Posaunenstelle, Leertext, Fackelhöhe, Zeitloch.* These compounds do not readily translate as such. In a kind of paradigmatic test, I've taken the options English offers—a possessive, a hyphen, separate words, and a single formation: "trumpets' place," "text-

---

16   After Böschenstein's 1977 article, see Heinz Michael Krämer, *Eine Sprache des Leidens: Zur Lyrik von Paul Celan* (Munich, 1979), 179-180; Peter Waterhouse, *Auf dem Weg zum "Kunst-Freien": Ammerkungen zur Utopie in der Lyrik Paul Celans* (Ph.D. diss., Vienna, 1984); and Hamburger's introduction, *Poems,* 29. A recent discussion of that poem, in Arnold Stadler, *Das Buch der Psalmen und die deutschsprachige Lyrik des 20. Jahrhunderts: Zu den Psalmen im Werk Bertolt Brechts und Paul Celans* (Cologne, 1989), 224-49, does refer "Die Posaunenstelle" to "Old Testament" sources rather than to the Johannine Apocalypse.

void," "torch height," "timehole."

The last of these makes a nearly imponderable compound, given the depths and heights of "Die Posaunenstelle." The poem's vertical dimension, which the Israeli critic Stéphane Mosès revealingly correlates with God and Moses descending and ascending Sinai,[17] finally does seat itself in time as well as space, thereby grounding the poem in originative events from Genesis and Exodus. This four-dimensional *Zeitloch* or "timehole" resembles *Zeitgehöft,* used as the title for Celan's posthumously collected poems, including "Die Posaunenstelle."[18] But where the word *Zeitgehöft,* "homestead of time," articulates some expectation of return and dwelling, *Zeitloch* brings a black hole to mind. In earlier poems, Celan had formed words such as *zeittief,* "time-deep," and *zeitleer,* "time-empty" (1:168,154). A 1963 poem bleakly affirms that the human voice can testify to time's severest ruptures: "Deep / in the time-crevasse, / by / honeycomb-ice / waits, a breath-crystal, / your irrefutable / witness" (2:31). Now "timehole" no less equivocally opens the late poem to some downward regress, a source and recourse that still may coincide with irremediable darkness and loss. And that is where *Zeitloch* leaves us, at the colon introducing a final imperative, which now turns the poem's reader into its auditor.

These closing words,

    hör dich ein
    mit dem Mund,

---

17   Mosès, *Spuren der Schrift,* 140.

18   *Zeitgehöft* (Frankfurt, 1976) is the title given to all of Celan's posthumously collected late poems, though he himself had attached it only to the first of three sheaves of them; "Die Posaunenstelle" occurs in the second sheaf. The collection appears in *GW,* vol. 3.

with three almost equally stressed monosyllables per line, embody a
prosodic imperative for their translator as well, beneath (and because
of) what they explicitly ask from the poet or audience:

> hear deep in
> with your mouth.

Perhaps the three-beat of the word *te-ki-ah* itself, the shofar blast,
makes me cleave to the German's staccato cadence and sound. Or
even more compellingly, a common Yiddish imperative makes itself
heard—*her dikh ayn,* "pay attention," "listen carefully"—so that
the German *hör dich ein* may actually be a calque, standing in for
its older, homier cousin tongue voided in the mouths of nearly five
million speakers.

Constraints such as these make one feel that no rendering of
"hör dich ein" will quite do, and that some extra push is called for.
Does the English "hear deep in" overdo Celan's simpler reflexive
construction, "hear yourself in"? As to whether the word I've added
here, "deep," aptly or ineptly echoes "tief" four lines earlier, "deep
in the glowing / text-void," that question carries beyond the literal
reach of the poem, as if both German and English versions were now
converging toward some point still out of hearing. To approach that
point, my second "deep" doubly bonds the translation"—a kind of
palimpsest—to its original or pretext, such as to bring the cognate
languages into an ongoing process.

What response does this closing imperative call for, from
the belated poet facing a "glowing text-void" as from the listener
facing that plus the poem itself? What will it feel like to hear "with
your mouth"? To seal the New Testament connection, a German
interpreter of Celan has cited chapter 10 of Revelation, where Saint

John eats a "little book" the angel gives him "and it was sweet in my mouth like honey."[19] Yet this incident derives from the Hebrew prophet Ezekiel in Babylon, to whom God spoke from a brightness: "Hear what I say unto thee...open thy mouth, and eat that which I give thee." Ezekiel ate a scroll written all over with lamentations, "and it was in my mouth like honey for sweetness" (2.8-3.3). With destruction and exile latent in the "timehole" of Celan's poem, this text from Ezekiel has a way to "hear deep in / with your mouth." Again a Hebraic source intervenes near the Christian Apocalypse, as when Celan's word *Posaunen* could call up the shofar in Exodus and Joshua and Isaiah sooner than in Revelation.

The "voice of the shofar"—at the Sinai covenant, on the Temple Mount for Sabbath, or yearly during the Rosh Hashanah and Yom Kippur rituals—is heart at a break in time announcing theophany, revelation, renewal. In "Die Posaunenstelle" the colon and stanza break after "Zeitloch" open a blank line or "text-void"—a "timehole," as it were—that both invites and might engulf response. Every lyric Celan wrote poises at such a point, and he kept that poise when he spoke his poems with acutest enunciation. To "hear deep in" (he prized a maxim that Walter Benjamin applied to kafka, "Attentiveness is the natural prayer of the soul"; 3:198)—to "hear deep in" to the voided covenant, to the abyss opened under Celan's own time, would seem task enough. Of itself and its hearer, "Die Posaunenstelle" unremittingly asks more: breath, speech, response, a further voice.

---

19   Krämer, *Sprache des Leidens,* 180.

ET IN ARCADIA ASTRA

G.C. Waldrep

*

You have to go outside Celan to read Celan. But this is not possible: any poem by Celan is a singularity. There is no "outside."

As readers, we split the atom. There is power in this. Also the end of the world.

*

In Celan's poems, the "you" is a congeries of points, of fragments, brief, unstable fields of reference and address. It has no independent existence beyond the scope the poet's attention lends. It is like a constellation: essentially, an act of naming, which is to say, a point of view. All the "you" possesses as its own is the poet's vantage, its act of (self-) definition.

And like the constellations, a story.

*

Celan's later poems eschew traditional narrative because they excuse the reader from nothing. *Nothing.* They offer no story, no lamp to light the way, no guiding thread. We want to be led into the maze of consciousness-through-experience by narrative, and then back out again. Celan's poems refuse to do this. They are exercises in a radical clarity, which is to say, choice.

Most literature exists first and foremost as entertainment, that is, as insulation against the radical clarity volition demands. Celan's poems force the reader, line by line, to choose, even at the most basic levels of meaning: the grapheme, the word.

271

And what is more terrifying, in the end, than choice?

*

God dies into God, Jabès writes. And the poem into the poem?

*

Celan is precisely the point where metaphor fails language, or rather, fails the human *experience* of language, experience-in-language. Celan's poetry is "like" nothing. It can be compared to nothing, because it self-consciously undercuts all bases for comparison, every easy empathy.

It can be argued that the most basic literary devices—metaphor, simile, personification, allusion—exist to finesse the radical gap between self and Other, between the Otherhood of a speaking self and the essential discretion of an external text. In this they are tools, which is to say, falsehoods.

Celan has his hands already full with an unreliable tool, the German language. Any language: the tool is on loan to him. He does not know who truly owns it, to what or whom it has pledged allegiance. He knows all too well the uses to which it can be put by others.

To use the literary devices of language—of literature—as facilitators of empathy is at best a hapless undertaking, at worst an exercise in damnation. Empathy is suspect. We do not know beforehand which doors we are opening. Do you want to empathize with the Nazi regime, that particular set of usages to which a particular language had been put?

One could argue that the Nazi regime represented a dramatic

depersonalization of the language, a denaturing of the tongue. On the contrary, Celan might counter. What the Nazis did to German was all too personal.

"The fact is," writes Oppen, "in the end either you want to kill a German, or else you do not."

*

To what extent is poetry a theology of expectation? And just what sort of expectation are we talking about? Celan's poems are not only discrete in their wounds (the wounds they tear in language; the wounds language tears in experience, into the white page) but also in that they seem to gesture, to yearn towards an outside they neither believe in nor permit.

But then, at the point where Celan's poems begin to make paratactic sense, the poet makes himself an absence, an articulate blank. Does the reader disappear too?

*

I tell my students one gauge of the greatness of any literary text is the extent to which it penetrates our dreaming. My students resist this. It is not, they argue, an objective measure. It is not even a criterion of consciousness, except insofar as we remember dreams. Dreams are notoriously inexact, doubtful, fragmentary, contradictory. And of course I, as a dreamer, can never be sure of what you dream, or what you say you dream.

The poems of Celan are different. A few are dreamy, but none are dreams.

They are not, as so many poems seem to be, apparent translations of dreams (of nearly-inaccessible experience) into the

273

living consciousness of articulation, of language.

The late poems of Celan are fragments not of dreaming but of waking, rescued from the experience of an Othered consciousness at the far edges of estrangement. They are what dreams remember of our waking lives, each night at the onset of dreaming.

*

Not *consequence,* or *inconsequence,* but something else— *deconsequence*?

*

When I dream of Celan, it is in the mesh of oppositions, of an experience of consciousness reduced radically to obstruction and interstice. *Dein goldenes Haar, Marguerite, dein aschenes Haar, Shulamith.* The poems are not so much *myths* of experience as a shorthand, perhaps even a rhythm of experience, a consciousness-pulse, a hum.

It is not that Celan's poems are distractions; it is that they are distracted. From what?

*

It is, of course, absurd to assign names and stories to arrangements of stars, immense flaming balls of gas and light only apparent—visible, in that arrangement—from a single point in space. Travel anywhere else in the universe and "Orion" disappears. But: travel anywhere else in the universe of the human mind, and *we* disappears, too.

This would be reassuring if it were possible. That is why the names, the stories we assign the stars are invented, or far in the past, or both. They—the names, the stories—are scapegoats.

Celan looked into language and saw words, even syllables, strewn against an infinite darkness. It was all very distant, an astronomer losing eyesight in old age, a child looking down the mouth of a stone well. Immense distances between each word, each syllable, each letter.

*

Poetry is like entering a room someone or something has just left. Maybe it's a homey sitting room, fire crackling in the grate, inviting; maybe it's a sumptuously-appointed hall. Either way, you're the only one there. There was music playing, but it's quiet now. You've missed someone or something important by minutes, perhaps even seconds. The telephone has just been ringing—somehow you know this—and you pick it up, just in time to hear *click*.

All poets, then, are messianic, or rather all poems: still waiting for something that may have already moved on, or may yet abide, immanent. Only: we live in bodies. One must occupy somehow. As men and women we may experience a lively expectation, but the poem, caged in language, knows only the precinct of its cage. Each poem inhabits its own version of Plato's cave.

The poem exists as *incarnation-in-language,* if such a thing were possible. (The flesh of language, a word made flesh.) It bodies-forth in language, it achieves a particular synthesis of spirit and substance we call "poetry." But it cannot save a man, because it cannot die and rise again from death on our behalf.

*

Jabès again: "Every work cancels the dark. Every work is a hymn from the other side of memory to a memory that is spellbound. Beauty is death's gift to vulgar life so that it can live in beauty."

René Char puts it another way: "However long its tether, poetry wounds itself in our hands as we are wounded, in turn, by its escapings."

*

Tell me a story, the poem whispers to the reader from its vast Outside, its not-place, its (restless) not-thought. Its *Niemandsrose* strobing the velate screen of the mind.

*

If we looked up into the night sky and saw ourselves in that cold distancing it would be unbearable.

We look up into the night sky, and this is what we see.

Appendix

THE MERIDIAN

Paul Celan

Speech on the occasion of the award of the Georg Büchner Prize

Ladies and Gentlemen!

Art, you will recall, is a puppet-like, iambic, five-footed and—mythology confirms this in the reference to Pygmalion and his creature—a childless being.

In this guise art forms the subject of a conversation that takes place in a room, not in the Conciergerie prison, a conversation that could go on endlessly, we feel, if nothing intervened.

Something does intervene.

Art returns. It returns in another work by Georg Büchner, in W*oyzeck*, among other, nameless people and—if I may bring in a phrase coined by Moritz Heimann about *Danton's Death*—in "a thunderstorm's more livid light." The very same art, even in this wholly different age, turns up again, presented by a carnival barker, not linked to the "glowing," "surging," "glittering" creation in that conversation, but alongside the creature and the nada this creature "has on"—art appears this time in the shape of a monkey, but it's the same, we recognize it right away by the "coat and trousers."

And it also comes to us, does art, in a third work of Büchner's in *Leonce and Lena.* Here time and lighting are not recognizable, we're "on the flight to paradise," "all clocks and calendars are soon to be "smashed" or "prohibited"—but shortly before this, "two persons, one of each sex," are produced, "two world-renowned robots have arrived," and a man proclaiming himself "perhaps the third and most remarkable of them all" challenges us "in a rasping tone" to marvel at what's before our eyes: "Nothing but art and mechanism, nothing but pasteboard and watch springs."

Art appears here with a larger entourage than before, but visibly among its own kind: it is the same art, the art we already know. —Valerio is just another name for the barker.

Art, ladies and gentlemen, with everything belonging and still to be added to it, is also a problem, indeed an elusive one, tough and long-lived, which is to say eternal.

A problem that allows someone mortal, Camille, and someone understandable only through his death, Danton, to string words onto words. It feels good to talk about art.

But when the talk concerns art, there's always someone who is present and...not really listening.

More precisely: someone who hears and listens and looks... and then doesn't know what the talk was about. But who hears the speaker, "sees him speak," perceives language and form and, at the same time—who could doubt it, here in the realm of this work—at the same time perceives Breath as well, that is, direction and destiny.

This someone, as you've realized, who is quoted so often and not at all by chance, coming before you in every new year—this someone is Lucile.

What intervened during the conversation pushes heedlessly on, it arrives with us at the Place de la Révolution, "the carts are driven up and stop."

The passengers are there, in full force, Danton, Camille, the others. Even here they all find words, artful words, and put them to good use, they talk of a communal "going-to-our-death" and here Büchner need only quote, Fabre wants to be able to die "twice over," everyone is at his best, —only some voices, "a few"—nameless—

"voices" observe that this has all "happened before" and is "tedious."

And here, where everything comes to its end, in longlasting moments as Camille—no, not him, not really him but a co-traveler—, as this Camille theatrically, one might almost say iambically, dies a death that, two scenes later, we only then discern as his own, through a word that's strange to him yet so close; as all around Camille, pathos and proverbialism confirm the triumph of "puppet" and "wire," here comes Lucile, blind to art, the same Lucile for whom language is something personal and perceptible, once again with her sudden "Long live the King!"

After all those words uttered on the rostrum (it's the scaffold)—what a word!

It is a counter-word, a word that snaps the "wire," a word that no longer bows to "history's loiterers and parade-horses," it is an act of freedom. It is a step.

Certainly this sounds—and in view of what I'm venturing to say about it now, today, there may be no coincidence—this sounds at first like a profession of faith in the "ancien régime."

But here—you'll allow someone who grew up with the writings of Peter Kropotkin and Gustav Landauer to stress this explicitly—here there's no homage to monarchy or to any so preservable Yesterday.

Homage here is to the Majesty of the Absurd, testifying to human presence.

And that, ladies and gentlemen, has no fixed name once and for all time, yet it is, I believe...poetry.

"—alas, Art!" I'm caught, you see, on this word of Camille's.

I'm fully aware we can read this word one way or another,

give it differing accents: the acute of the contemporary, the *grave* accent of history (and literary history too), the circumflex—marking length—of the eternal.

I give it—there's no other choice left me—, I give it the acute.

Art—"alas, Art": besides its ability to transmute, it has the gift of ubiquity: it can be found in Lenz as well, here too—I allow myself to stress this—as in *Danton's Death*, an episode.

"At table Lenz was again in good spirits: they talked about literature, he was on his home turf..."
"...The feeling that what's been created possesses life outweighs both of these and is the sole criterion in matters of art..."

Here I've extracted only two sentences, my bad conscience over the *grave* accent forbids my not calling your attention to this right away, —this passage touches on literary history above all, we must read it together with the conversation from *Danton's Death* cited above, here Büchner's aesthetic finds expression, from here, leaving Büchner's *Lenz* fragment behind, we get to Reinhold Lenz, author of "Notes on Theater," and through him, the historical Lenz, further back to Mercier's "Elargisse l'Art," literally so fruitful, this passage opens vistas, anticipating Naturalism, Gerhart Hauptmann, here the social and political roots of Büchner's work are to be sought and found.

Ladies and gentlemen, that I don't let this go unmentioned eases my conscience, if only temporarily, but at the same time it also shows you, and thus troubles my conscience afresh, —it shows you I can't free my mind of something that seems linked to art.

281

I am seeking it here, too, in *Lenz*—I'll permit myself to call it to your attention.

Lenz, that is, Büchner, has—"alas, Art"—scornful words for "Idealism" and its "wooden puppets." He sets them off, and here those unforgettable lines on the "life of the humblest" occur, the "quiverings," the "intimations," the "subtle, scarcely discernible play of the features," —he sets them off against what is natural and creaturely. And this concept of art he illustrates by means of an experience:

"Yesterday, as I was walking up along the valley rim, I saw two girls sitting on a rock: one was doing up her hair, the other helping her; and the golden hair hung down, and the pale serious face, yet so young, and the black dress, and the other girl taking such pains. The Old German School's finest, most intimate pictures can scarcely give an idea of it. At times one might wish to be a Medusa's head, so as to turn such a group into stone and call people over."

Ladies and gentlemen, please take note: "One might wish to be a Medusa's head," so as to...grasp the natural as natural by means of art!

One might wish to, it says, not: *I* might.

This means stepping out of what is human, betaking oneself to a realm that is uncanny yet turned toward what's human—the same realm where the monkey, the robots and thereby...alas, art too seems to be at home.

This is not the historical Lenz speaking, but Büchner's, here it's Büchner's voice we've heard, here too: art for him retains something uncanny.

Ladies and gentlemen, I have put on the acute accent; I would not deceive you any more than myself, that with my question about art and poetry—one among many questions—that with this question I must have gone to Büchner of my own (if not my free) will, to seek out his question.

But as you can see: Valerio's "rasping tone," whenever art comes forth, cannot be missed.

Probably these are—Büchner's voice forces me to this conjecture—among the oldest forms of the uncanny. That I dwell on them so stubbornly today has likely to do with the air—the air we have to breathe.

Isn't there, I must now ask, in Georg Büchner, the poet of the creature, an only half spoken, perhaps, only half conscious but no less radical—or for that very reason in the most literal sense a radical calling-into-question of art, a calling-into-question from this direction? A calling-into-question that all poetry today must come back to, if it wants to go on questioning? In other words (to leap ahead a little): May we, as happens in many places nowadays, proceed from art as from something already given and implicitly assumed, should we, to put it bluntly, above all—let's say—be thinking Mallarmé through to the end?

I've reached ahead, reached beyond—not far enough, I know—, I'll get back to Büchner's *Lenz*, to that (episodic) conversation carried on "at table" when Lenz "was in good spirits."

Lenz talked a long time, "now smiling, now serious." And now, with the conversation over, it's said about him—that is, about the one concerned with questions of art, but likewise about Lenz the artist: "He had quite forgotten himself."

283

I think of Lucile when I read that. I read: *He*, he himself.

Whoever keeps art before his eyes and in his mind—here I'm thinking of *Lenz*—has forgotten himself. Art creates I-distantness. Art in a certain direction demands a certain distance, a certain path.

And poetry? Poetry, which still has to take the path of art? Then we'd really have the path to the Medusa's head and the robot.

Now I'm not seeking a way out, I'm only questioning further, in the same direction and also, I believe, in the direction of the *Lenz* fragment.

Perhaps—I'm only asking—perhaps poetry, like art, is going with a self-forgotten I toward the uncanny and the strange, and is again—but where? but in what place? but with what? but as what?—setting itself free?

Then art would be the distance poetry must cover—no less, no more.

I know, there are other shorter paths. But poetry too hurries ahead of us at times. La poésie, elle aussi, brûle nos étapes.

I shall leave the self-forgotten man, concerned with art, the artist. I believe I have encountered poetry in Lucile, and Lucile perceives language as form and direction and breath—: I'm seeking the same thing here in this work of Büchner's, I seek Lenz himself, seek him—as a person, I seek his form: for the sake of poetry's place, for the setting free, for the step.

Büchner's Lenz, ladies and gentlemen, remained a fragment. Should we seek out the historical Lenz, to learn what direction this existence had?

"His existence was an urgent burden for him. —So he lived on..." Here the story breaks off.

But poetry, like Lucile, does attempt to see the direction form takes, poetry hurries ahead. We know *where* he lives on, how he lives *on*.

"Death," we read in a 1909 book on Jakob Michael Reinhold Lenz published in Leipzig—it comes from the pen of a Moscow lecturer by the name M. N. Rosanow— "Death the Redeemer did not make him wait long. The night of 23–24 May 1792, Lenz was found lifeless in a Moscow street. A nobleman paid for his burial. His final resting place remains unknown."

So *he* had lived *on*.

He: the true Lenz, Büchner's, Büchner's figure, the person we perceived on the story's first page, the Lenz who "went walking in the mountains on the 20th of January," he—not the artist and one concerned with questions of art, but he as an I.

Will we now perhaps find the place where the strangeness was, the place where a person was able to set himself free as an—estranged— I? Will we find such a place, such a step?

"...only it sometimes troubled him that he could not walk on his head." —That is him, Lenz. That is, I believe, him and his step, him and his "Long live the King."

"...only it sometimes troubled him that he could not walk on his head."

Whoever walks on his head, ladies and gentlemen, whoever walks on his head has heaven as an abyss beneath him.

Ladies and gentlemen, nowadays it's common to blame poetry for its "obscurity." —Allow me here, abruptly—but hasn't something suddenly come open?—allow me to cite a phrase of Pascal's, a phrase I read a little while ago in Leo Shestov: "Ne nous reprochez pas le manque de clarté puisque nous en faisons profession!" That obscurity is, I believe, if not congenital, then the obscurity associated with poetry for the sake of an encounter, by a perhaps self-devised distance or strangeness.

But perhaps, in one and the same direction, there are two kinds of strangeness—chockablock.

Lenz—that is, Büchner—has gone one step further than Lucile. His "Long live the King" is no longer words, it is a frightful falling silent, it takes away his—also our—breath and word.

Poetry: that can signify an *Atemwende*, a Breathturn. Who knows, perhaps poetry follows its path—also the path of art—for the sake of such a breathturn? Perhaps, since strangeness—the abyss *and* the Medusa's head, the abyss *and* the robots—seems to lie in a single direction, perhaps poetry here succeeds in telling strangeness from strangeness, perhaps right here the Medusa's head shrinks, perhaps right here the robots break down—for this unique brief moment? Perhaps here, with the I—the estranged I set free *here* and in *such wise*—here perhaps yet some Other becomes free?

Perhaps from here on the poem is itself...and in this art-less, art-free way can now follow its other paths, including the paths of art—again and again?

Perhaps.

Perhaps we may say that every poem has its "20th of January" inscribed? Perhaps what's new for poems written today is just this: that here the attempt is clearest to remain mindful of such dates?

But don't we all date from such dates? And what dates do we ascribe ourselves to?

Yet the poem does speak! It remains mindful of its dates, yet—it speaks. Indeed it speaks only in its very selfmost cause.

But I think—and now this thought can hardly surprise you— I think a hope of poems has always been to speak in just this way in the cause of the *strange*—no, I can't use this word anymore—in just this way to speak *in the cause of an Other*—who knows, perhaps in the cause of a *wholly Other*.

This "who knows" I see I've now arrived at is the only thing I can add, for myself, today and here, to the old hopes.

Perhaps, I must tell myself now—perhaps even a meeting between this "wholly Other"—I'm using a familiar term here—and a not all that distant, a quite near "other" becomes thinkable— thinkable again and again.

A poem's lingerings or longings—a word related to the creature—touch such thoughts.

No one can say how long the breath-pause—the longing and the thought—will last. "Speed," which was always "outside," has gained speed; a poem knows this, but it makes straight for that "Other" which it deems reachable, free-able, perhaps empty and thus turned—let's say, like Lucile—toward it, toward the poem.

Certainly the poem, the poem today shows—and this I think has only indirectly to do with not-to-be-underestimated difficulties of word choice, with the sharper fall of syntax or heightened sense of ellipses—the poem unmistakably shows a strong bent toward falling silent.

It holds on—after so many extreme formulations, allow me this one too—the poem holds on at the edge of itself; so as to exist, it

287

ceaselessly calls and hauls itself from its Now-no-more back into its Ever-yet.

But this Ever-yet could be only an act of speaking. Not simply language and probably not just verbal "correspondence" either.

But actualized language, set free under the sign of a radical individuation, which at the same time stays mindful of the limits drawn by language, the possibilities opened by language.

This ever-yet of poems can only be found in a poem by someone who does not forget that he speaks from the angle of inclination of his very being, his creatureliness.

Then a poem would be—even more clearly than before—the language-become-form of a single person and, following its inmost nature, presentness and presence.

The poem is lonely. It is lonely and underway. Whoever writes one stays mated with it.

But in just this way doesn't the poem stand, right here, in an encounter—*in the mystery of an encounter?*

The poem wants to reach an Other, it needs this Other, it needs an Over-against. It seeks it out, speaks toward it.

For the poem making toward an Other, each thing, each human being is the form of this Other.

The attentiveness a poem devotes to all it encounters, with its sharper sense of detail, outline, structure, color, but also of "quiverings" and "intimations"—all this, I think, is not attained by an eye vying (or conniving) with constantly more perfect instruments. Rather, it is a concentration that stays mindful of all our dates.

"Attentiveness"—allow me here to quote a saying by Malebranche from Walter Benjamin's Kafka essay—"Attentiveness is the natural prayer of the soul."

A poem—under what conditions!—becomes the poem of someone (ever yet) perceiving, facing phenomena, questioning and addressing these phenomena; it becomes conversation—often despairing conversation.

What is addressed takes shape only in the space of this conversation, gathers around the I addressing and naming it. But what's addressed and is now become a Thou through naming, as it were, also brings along its otherness into this present. Even in a poem's here and now—the poem itself really has only this one, unique, momentary present—even in this immediacy and nearness it lets the Other's ownmost quality speak: its time.

When we speak with things this way, we are always dealing with the question of their Whence and Whither: with a question "staying open," "coming to no end," pointing into the open and void and free—we are far outside.

A poem, I believe, is searching for this place too.

A poem?

A poem with is images and tropes?

Ladies and gentlemen, what I am really speaking about when I speak from *this* direction, in *this* direction, with *these* words about a poem—no, about *the* poem?

I am speaking about a poem that does not exist!

The absolute poem—no, that certainly doesn't exist, that can't exist!

But there is, with every real poem, with the most undemanding poem, there is this unavoidable question, this unheard-of demand.

And then what would the images be?

Something perceived and to be perceived only now and only here, once, again and again once. And so a poem would be the place where all tropes and metaphors will be carried ad absurdum.

Topos research?

By all means! But in light of what's to be explored: in light of U-topia.

And human beings? And creatures?

In this light.

What questions! What demands!

It is time to turn back.

Ladies and gentlemen, I am at the end—I am back at the beginning.

Élargissez l'Art! With its old, with its new uncanniness, this question steps up to us. I went toward Büchner with it—I thought to find it there again.

I even had an answer ready, a "Lucilesque" counter-word, I wanted to set something opposite, to be there with my contradiction:

Enlarge art?

No. But with art go into your very selfmost straits. And set yourself free.

Here, too, in your presence, I've taken this path. It was a circle.

Art, thus also the Medusa's head, the mechanism, the robots, the uncanny strangeness so hard to tell apart, in the end perhaps really only *one* strangeness—art lives on.

Twice, with Lucile's "Long live the King" and when heaven as an abyss opened up under Lenz, the *Atemwende* seemed to be there, in the Breathturn. Perhaps also when I tried to make toward that occupiable distance which finally became visible only in the figure of Lucile. And once, given the attentiveness devoted to things and creatures, we even got near something open and free. And at last near utopia.

Poetry, ladies and gentlemen—: this speaking endlessly of mere mortality and uselessness!

Ladies and gentlemen, allow me once again, since I'm back at the beginning, to ask the same thing as briefly as possible and from another direction.

Ladies and gentlemen, several years ago I wrote a little quatrain—this is it:

"Voices from the nettle path: / *Come on your hands to us.* / Whoever is alone with the lamp / has only his hand to read from."

And a year ago, in memory of a failed encounter in the Engadin, I set down a little story in which I had a man "like Lenz" walked through the mountains.

In both instances I'd begun writing from a "20th of January," from my "20th of January."

It was...myself I encountered.

Then does one, in thinking of poems, does one walk such paths with poems? Are these paths only by-paths, bypaths from thou to thou? Yet at the same time, among how many other paths, they're also paths on which language gets a voice, they are encounters, paths of a voice to a perceiving Thou, creaturely paths, sketches of existence perhaps, sending oneself ahead toward oneself, in search of oneself....A kind of homecoming.

Ladies and gentlemen, I am coming to the end—with the acute accent I had to use, I'm coming to the end of...*Leonce and Lena.*

And here, with the last two words of this work, I must take care.

 I must guard myself, like Karl Emil Franzos, the editor of that "First Complete Critical Edition of Georg Büchner's Collected Works and Posthumous Manuscripts," published by Sauerländer eighty-one years ago in Frankfurt am Main—I must guard against reading—*like my countryman Karl Emil Franzos whom I've rediscovered here*—the word "accommodating," which is accepted today, as if it were "coming"!

 And yet: Doesn't *Leonce and Lena* itself have quotations marks invisibly around the words? Quotation marks to be understood not as goose feet, perhaps, but rather as rabbit ears, not unanxiously listening out beyond themselves and the words?

 From this standpoint, from "accommodating," though also in light of utopia, I'll now undertake topos research.

 I am seeking the region that Reinhold Lenz and Karl Emil Franzos come from, whom I encountered on my path here and via Georg Büchner. I also seek—for I'm back again where I began—the place of my own origin.

 I am seeking all of that with an inexact because uneasy finger on the map—on a children's map, I must admit.

 None of these places is to be found, they do not exist, but I know where, especially now, they would have to exist, and....I find something!

Ladies and gentlemen, I find something that comforts me a little at having taken, in your presence, this impossible path, this path of the impossible.

I find something that binds and that leads to encounter, like a poem.

I find something—like language—immaterial yet earthly, terrestrial, something circular, returning upon itself by way of both poles and thereby—happily—even crossing the tropics (and tropes): I find...a *meridian*.

With you and Georg Büchner and the State of Hesse I believe I've just touched it again.

Ladies and gentlemen, a high honor has been conferred on me today. I shall be able to remember that along with people whose person and work mean an encounter for me, I am the bearer of a prize that commemorates Georg Büchner.

I give you heartfelt thanks for this distinction, heartfelt thanks for this moment and this encounter.

I thank the State of Hesse. I thank the city of Darmstadt. I thank the German Academy of Language and Literature.

I thank the President of the German Academy of Language and Literature, I thank you, my dear Hermann Kasack.

My dear Marie Luise Kaschnitz, I thank you.

Ladies and gentlemen, I thank you for your presence.

I have come to you in Israel because I needed to.

As seldom with such a feeling, I have the strongest sense, after all I've seen and heard, of having done the right thing—not just for me alone, I hope.

I think I have a notion of what Jewish loneliness can be, and I recognize as well, among so many things, a thankful pride in every green thing planted here that's ready to refresh anyone who comes by; just as I take joy in every newly earned, self-discovered, fulfilled word that rushes up to strengthen those who turn toward it—I take that joy in these times of growing self-alienation and mass conformity everywhere. And I find here, in this outward and inward landscape, much of the force for truth, the self-evidentness, and the world-open uniqueness of great poetry. And I believe I've been conversing with those who are calmly, confidently determined to stand firm in what is human.

I am thankful for all that, and I thank you.

translated from the German by John Felstiner

ACKNOWLEDGMENTS

"god of rooms" by Jean Valentine. Published with permission of the author.

"Of Strangeness That Wakes Us" by Ilya Kaminsky. Published with permission of
the author.

"Paul Celan: Translating the Poet" by Eavan Boland. Published with permission of
the author.

"Paul Celan" by Cid Corman. Reprinted with permission of Rob Arnold for the
Estate of Cid Corman.

"False Sail" by Anne Carson. Published with permission of the author.

"For a Long Time: Into Whisperings and Rustlings" by Gennady Aygi, translated by
Peter France. Published with permission of Peter France.

"Celan's Breakthrough Book," by David Young. Published with permission of the
author.

"Northtrue. Southbright" and "Meditations on Them and the Earth Inside Them
That They Dug" by Dan Beachy-Quick. Published with permission of the
author.

"THE BOOK OF LUAP NALEC" by Pierre Joris. Published with permission of the
author.

"Being and the Other: On Paul Celan" by Emmanuel Levinas, translated by Stephen
Melville. Published with permission of the translator.

"Shibboleth," Part III, by Jacques Derrida, translated by Joshua Wilner and Thomas
Dutoit, from *Sovereignties in Question: The Poetics of Paul Celan.*
Reprinted with permission of Johns Hopkins University Press.

"Vigilous, Reel: Desire (A)s Accusation" by Nathanaël (formerly Nathalie
Stephens). Reprinted with permission of the author.

"Lorine Niedecker Harmonizing with Paul Celan" by Elizabeth Robinson.
Published with permission of the author.

"Paul Celan and Language" by Jacques Derrida, translated by Pierre Joris.
Copyright the Estate of Jacques Derrida. Published with permission of
Pierre Joris and the Estate of Jacques Derrida.

"The Memory of Words" by Edmond Jabès, translated by Pierre Joris. Copyright
the Estate of Edmond Jabes. Published with permission of Pierre Joris and
the Estate of Edmond Jabès.

295